Devotional Stories for Little Folks, Too

Nancy Nicholson

For Little Folks
Dresden, Ohio

Copyright © 2007 Nancy Nicholson

Devotional Stories for Little Folks, Too is under copyright. All rights reserved. No part of this book may be reproduced in any form by any means—electronic, mechanical, or graphic—without prior written permission. Thank you for honoring copyright law.

Scripture quotations are excerpted from: *Ignatius Bible, Revised Standard Version-Catholic Edition*, © 1965, 1966 by Division of Christian Education of the National Council of the Churches of Christ in the United States of America. Used by permission. All rights reserved.

ISBN: 978-0-9771236-1-2

For Little Folks
P.O. Box 571
Dresden, OH 43821

Distributed by Catholic Heritage Curricula
P.O. Box 125, Twain Harte, CA 95383
1-800-490-7713 www.chcweb.com

Cover and interior design by Osprey Design,
www.ospreydesign.com

Dedicated

to

St. Joseph,

powerful patron of families;

and to the Weathers' family,

who were not 'from St. Joe,' yet

under his protection still

Any resemblance, real or imagined, between the characters in these stories and family members, is coincidental,

mostly.

Contents

Introduction, *vi*
As for Me and My House, *1*
'C' is for 'Truck'? *6*
'Muffin' Sandwiches, *11*
The Wise Man, *16*
It Seemed So Good, *20*
'My Special Time', *25*
Family Building Blocks, *29*
Tasting Temptation, *36*
Whining Mosquitos, *41*
God's Wise Order, *46*
Created for My Glory, *51*
Living Examples, *56*
A Log Truck for Jesus, *61*
Mending More than a Top, *67*
Much More than a Tree, *74*
Seth's Pane-ful Accident, *80*
Happy Holy-days, *85*
In God's Good Time, *90*
Jesus' Chore Chart, *95*
Becca Digs a Pit, *99*

Living the Gospel, Part I, *106*
Living the Gospel, Part II, *112*
Judging Where to Walk, *118*
Will You Trust Me?, *124*
Too Much of a Good Thing, *131*
He Saw, and He Knows, *135*
Sharing 'Most Everything, *141*
Steps Leading Nowhere, *146*
Big Rivers to Cross, *152*
Because They Do, *158*
Home, Sweet Home, *162*
Looking Inside, *168*
Joy to My Youth, *173*
A Gift that Won't Break, *179*
Squeaky Clean, *184*
Hide and Seek, *188*

Answer Key, *194*
Topical Index, *199*

Introduction

These little stories may be used for daily devotions, as gentle examples for moral training, or for primary reading practice and enjoyment.

Utilizing this volume for morning devotions may set the tone for the day and allow the child time to ponder the teaching offered, putting it into practice as his day unfolds under Our Lord's direction.

For those seeking story topics to reinforce moral training, this volume features a topical index. In addition, included with each story are relevant quotations from Holy Scripture and the *Catechism of the Catholic Church*. If stories are presented on a weekly basis, one may wish to copy these quotations and post prominently.

To encourage vocabulary development and reading comprehension, new vocabulary and comprehension questions are found at the end of each tale. Comprehension questions are also designed to stimulate thoughtful discussion of presented topics.

Whether your family opens this volume for daily devotions, to reinforce godly principles, or for the sheer relief of reading about another family dealing with similar challenges, we pray that the Holy Spirit will add His good measure of life and light to each reading.

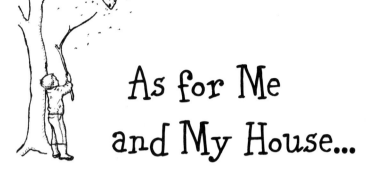

As for Me and My House...

Wham! Greg's **sturdy** hammer slammed down on the golden dandelion. A sleepy bee that had been resting on the flower shot into the sky.

Greg jumped to his feet. He waved the hammer at the puffy clouds and shouted, "I'll get you next time, Mr. Bee!"

Why, you may wonder, was Greg trying to hammer a bee? But then, if you are wondering that, maybe you haven't met Greg?

Let me introduce you to the Peterson children. Seth, the eldest, was nearly ten. Next came Meg, age eight, followed by Greg, six, and Becca, four.

The Peterson family lived in the country. Behind their home ran a creek with stick-choked beaver dams and favorite fishing holes. Wooded hills rose just beyond the creek. Cows shared a grassy pasture with **battered** bicycles, wagons, and a lop-sided clubhouse. The Peterson's big back yard spilled over with somersaulting children and scratching chickens, bright dandelions and humming bees. Their busy yard was also dotted with odd-looking dents, where Greg's worn hammer had left its mark.

You see, that past summer, the Peterson family had been for a walk in the shady woods behind their home. Meg had noticed a small hole in the dirt next to the path. As she bent over the opening, a yellow-jacket wasp sprang out and stung poor Meg.

Dad had warned the rest of the children to stay away from the dangerous hole. Of course, Greg had to see exactly where the opening was.

As he later explained while Mom was putting an ice cube on the swollen sting above his eye, "But I *had* to look at the hole, 'cuz if I didn't look at it, how would I know what hole not to look at?"

And that's how Greg's **private** war on any insect unlucky enough to look like a bee had begun.

Let's move ahead in our story, to join the Petersons at church.

Every First Friday, homeschooling families gathered there for Holy Mass and Adoration. It was a quiet time, a peaceful time. Seth and Meg loved to squeeze their eyes shut and imagine all their heavenly friends, the angels and saints, crowding the church with them, unseen, but very real. In that peaceful, holy time of Adoration, Seth and Meg visited with Jesus, their Best Friend.

That day, Father's homily had been about how important it is for Catholic families to choose God above everything else.

"Choose today whom you will serve," Father had said. That meant choosing God's ways, choosing to do good things, even when it was hard. It meant being kind to all, but following the right friends, friends who will lead in the right direction.

After Adoration, the children played together in the baseball field, or in the grove of trees at its edge, next to the parish hall. Sometimes, the girls skipped rope or played hopscotch while the older boys tossed a football.

At the moment, Seth and his friends were playing catch. Meg and her friends had chalked hopscotch squares on the sidewalk, and were teaching the pre-school girls where to hop.

In the tree grove at field's edge, Greg was showing the pre-school boys how to poke under fallen branches to find slugs.

"Then you put a slug on the end of a stick and make it fly, like this." Greg held a slug-tipped stick over his shoulder and then whipped it forward.

"Ooooohhh," said the little boys.

As Greg watched the slug rocket through the trees, he was surprised to see a football hanging from an overhead branch. No, on second **glance**, it wasn't quite the right shape for a football, and it looked sort of papery. Why, it was a hornets' paper nest!

Greg was so excited that he hit himself in the ear with his stick. "Ouch! It is too hard to get bees one at a time," he thought. "I bet that bee house has a bunch of bees that I could beat up with my stick. Why, if *everybody* has a stick, we could beat *all* the bees up!"

When Seth first heard voices shouting out Greg's name, he thought Greg was playing football with the big boys, like last month. Greg had run for a touchdown, but in the wrong direction. His team had yelled for him to turn around, but Greg thought they were cheering him on, so he didn't stop.

Now the shouting had turned to **shrieks** of fear. Seth turned to see the pre-school boys, some still waving sticks, come exploding out from under the trees. Greg was in the middle of the scattering group, racing for the church hall, with the angry hornets following close behind.

"Meg!" yelled Seth. "Go get the moms! And tell them to bring plenty of ice!"

That night Mrs. Peterson printed a simple note of **apology** on Greg's lined tablet paper. She told him to make several copies.

"And I think you need to say a special apology to little Chris the next time you see him, too," said Mom. "He was stung eleven times."

Greg was truly sorry. He wiped wet eyes on his shirt sleeve and picked up his well-chewed pencil. Printing was hard for him, even more so with the stings on his hands, but still he wrote a copy for each little boy who had been hurt.

Two hours later, when Greg had finished all his notes, Mother heard him leave the house. Greg soon returned with his hammer.

"Mommy?"

"Yes, Greg?"

"Can you wrap up my hammer and send it to Chris, too? He needs it more than I do."

"'...choose this day whom you will serve...as for me and my house, we will serve the LORD.'" —Jos. 24:15

New Vocabulary

sturdy: strong
battered: dented
private: in this case, belonging to only one person
glance: look
shriek: scream
apology: to say you're sorry

Questions

1. Why was the Peterson family at church on First Friday?
2. Father had said that part of choosing to follow God was choosing friends who will lead where?
3. What did Greg first think he saw in the tree? What did he really see?

'C' is for 'Truck'?

Seth made a face at his new history book and sighed. He folded his arms, and bent over in his chair until his forehead rested on the dining table's hard edge.

"I've never, never, flunked a test before, and now I've flunked two in a row!" he whispered unhappily. "And I'm spending so much time studying history that I'm six pages behind in my language book. I wish I never had to open these pages again!"

He pushed the language workbook to the end of the table where Becca and Greg were also 'doing school.' They were cutting colorful pictures from grocery ads and gluing them onto a sheet of cardboard. Soon they would have a big poster of letter 'C' words.

Becca's chubby little thumb and fingers struggled with the dull scissors. So far she had cut glossy pictures of carrots, cabbage, and cat food.

Greg, who was finding 'C' words too, had clipped photos of cookies, strawberry taffy, and a 4-wheel drive pick-up.

Poor Seth! He had too much to do! As Greg reached for the glue stick, an idea popped into his head. He could do something so his big brother would not have so much to study.

After first tasting the glue stick to make sure it was fresh, Greg set to work. Becca went on clipping pictures. Several minutes later, Greg gave Seth's workbook a satisfied pat and went back to looking for 'C' words in the truck ads.

Seth, with his head on the table, did not see Greg at work. Seth knew only that he was **miserable**. Before this year, he just had spelling tests. The spelling tests were so simple that he'd never had to study, and he still got all the words right.

But this year Seth had history tests, and history was different. He loved history. He had read books about Columbus and his trip to the Americas. Seth knew about Cortez and Mexico. He even knew about Crispus Attucks and the American Revolution. If he knew so much history, why was he doing so badly on the history tests?

"Why so **glum**, **chum**?" Dad, home early from work, set his steaming mug of coffee on the table and seated himself next to Seth.

"Oh, I just don't get it." Seth sadly lifted his head to face Dad. "I flunked the first test on chapter one, so I went back and studied that. Then I flunked the test on chapter two, so now I have to study that, too."

Dad moved his mug out of Greg's reach and asked, "You studied chapter one *after* you failed the test on chapter one? And now you're studying chapter two, *after* the test on chapter two?"

"Yes." Seth pulled the folded tests from the back of his book and handed them to Dad. "See? I missed all those questions."

Dad ran his finger down the line of red check marks. "Hmmm. Well, you didn't really flunk, but you did miss several. I think you do know the history. You just missed the dates, the days when everything happened. But it seems to me that history is much more than dates. History is about people who lived and died to bring Jesus' love and healing to the world. It is about brave men and women, wisdom and foolishness, sorrow and joy.

"So your real problem on these tests wasn't the wrong answers. You did poorly because you were looking backward, not forward."

"It's OK, Seth," offered Greg, stretching wide the neck of his T-shirt so all could see the shirt's tag in front. "I'm a backwards boy, too."

"You mean that I am studying for what is already over and done with," asked Seth, "something that I can't change?"

"Exactly. You can't change the past, but you can plan ahead to change the future."

"That's funny." Seth smiled a small smile. "That's what Fr. Dominic told me in confession.

"I was getting discouraged because I confess the same sins over and over. But Father told me that God doesn't see the same sins over and over. He sweeps them away each time I go to confession. He doesn't remember them because they are gone.

"Father said I can't change the past, but I can change the future. I can plan ways to stay away from what tempted me to sin before. If I plan, I can do better next time."

Dad handed the tests back to Seth. "That's it. Even better, the graces we receive in the sacraments help make us strong, to fight temptation and grow in holiness."

"Now, you still have to study for your tests, but why not plan for the *next* test, not the one that's already passed? If you do that, your grades will get better, and you'll quickly catch up on your work."

"Thanks, Dad." Seth stood and began to clear his books from the table. "Uh, Dad? One more problem: Greg just glued the pages of my language book together."

"I have swept away your transgressions like a cloud, and your sins like a mist..." —Is. 44:22

"...I will remember their sins no more." —Heb. 8:12

New Vocabulary

miserable: full of sadness, pitiful
glum: sad or miserable
chum: friend or buddy

Questions

1. Seth was having trouble with which tests?
2. Father said that you can't change the past, but you can change what?
3. After we confess our sins, how many of them does God remember?

'Muffin' Sandwiches

Early morning sunshine poured through the window into the bedroom that Meg and Becca shared. Golden sunbeams reached across the room and touched Becca's face. She opened her chocolate-brown eyes and blinked at the bright light.

The sun was out. Why, she would not have to stay inside again! All week it had rained and rained and rained, but now the gray days were over, and Becca could hardly wait to go outside.

Becca reached under her quilt for her favorite go-to-bed doll, Strawberry Muffin. 'Muffin' always, always went to bed with Becca. Beloved Muffin, from her wide, freckled smile, to her curly red locks and plump muffin body, took up little room in the bed, and was just the right size for Becca's small hands.

Unfortunately, 'Muffin' also fit very nicely between two slices of bread. Seth liked to tease Becca, that he was eating Muffin. And that's why, when Becca's searching hand came out from under the still-warm blankets, it was empty.

Now she remembered! Becca's usually cheerful face darkened. Seth had a snack last night. He had put Strawberry Muffin inside his peanut butter sandwich and pretended to gobble her up. Poor Muffin. She was covered with peanut butter, so Mama had put her in the wash. She was still wet when Becca went to bed last night, empty-handed, and angry.

"I am not going to talk to Seth, ever again," pouted Becca as she began to dress herself.

"Hmmmm?" Meg stretched and crawled from her nest of sheets and blankets. "Why aren't you going to talk to Seth?"

"He was eating Muffin. And I'm not going to play with him anymore, either."

"But Becca, Seth said he'd give you a ride in the wheelbarrow the next sunny day, and besides, you *like* playing with Seth!"

Even as Becca said, "No, I don't," she thought about how much fun it was when her big brother picked her up under her armpits and twirled around and around in circles. Her legs flew straight out and then they both got dizzy and fell down in a pile on the carpet and laughed. Seth was a fun big brother.

"No! I'm not even going to look at Seth." Becca stomped from the room to wash up before morning devotions and breakfast.

At the breakfast table, Mother noticed that Becca's face was nearly in her cereal bowl, while Seth looked downright **angelic**.

Mother raised her eyebrows almost to her hairline and stared from Seth to Becca and back again. "I can see that you two aren't getting along, and I'll bet it has something to do with Muffin."

"Muffins are delicious," said Seth innocently as he rose from the table. "I wish I had some for breakfast." Seth began inching toward the laundry room.

"No, Seth, no, Seth, no, Seth, NO!" Becca was out of her chair when Mother stopped both children.

"You two have carried this far enough. Seth, you need to stop teasing Becca beyond what she can take. Someone else needs to stop pouting and not let the sun go down on her anger. Forgiveness would be nice, too.

"Both of you go outside and sit on the porch steps. You can come in when you both agree to be friends again."

For a few moments, it was quiet on the porch. Seth thought about all the things he had planned to do that day. Sitting on the steps was not on his list.

He started singing a song he'd made up just for Becca, called 'Fleas in Her Nose.' It always made her laugh.

A tiny smile **flitted** across Becca's face.

Seth stopped singing. "I'm sorry I tried to eat Muffin," apologized Seth. "If you want, you can play with my train set all day. Anyway, haven't I been *nice* to you?"

"Not yet," grunted Becca.

"I know you went to bed mad last night, but if you stay mad, you will miss out on a happy day. This is the first sunny day we've had in a long time, and it might rain again tomorrow. We can be friends again, and then I can take you for a wheelbarrow ride," coaxed Seth.

"Will you turn me around in circles, too?"

"If I can have just a *little* bite of Muffin," teased Seth.

"No, Seth, no, Seth, no!," squealed Becca, but this time she was smiling. "OK, I forgive you. I don't want to be mad for a whole day."

"Happy is more fun than mad," agreed Seth. "Let's go ask Mom if we can hang Muffin in the sun to bake."

"...do not let the sun go down on your anger." —*Eph.* 4:26

'...forgive us our trespasses, as we forgive those who trespass against us...'

New Vocabulary

angelic: like an angel
flitted: fluttered

Questions

1. What does it mean to 'not let the sun go down on your anger'?
2. What might Becca have missed if she had not forgiven Seth?
3. If we do *not* forgive, what are we really saying when we ask God to forgive us in the same way that we forgive others?

The Wise Man

As the Peterson's **exited** the church after Sunday Mass, Mother and Greg spotted Mrs. Hansen in the crowd just ahead.

Greg raced to throw his arms around his favorite CCD teacher. Beaming up at her, he sang out, "Mrs. Hansen, I like you better with your dress on!"

Mother, turning bright red with embarrassment, hurried to explain. "What he means is that you often wear lovely pants outfits, but Greg thinks that your dresses are even prettier."

"I see," said Mrs. Hansen, a bit stiffly.

Mother grabbed Greg's hand and dragged him through the crowded parking lot to the van where the rest of the family was waiting.

"Mike," Mom groaned to Mr. Peterson as she slammed the van's door, "I don't know what to do with Greg. He has no control over his speech."

In the back seat, Greg had clicked his seat belt shut and opened his bag of car toys. He was now trying to see how many ping pong balls he could stuff into the van's ash tray.

"Greg," Seth noted, "you can't fit all those in the ash tray."

"Yes, you can," Greg answered as he leaned on the lid, "if you push hard enough."

Meg wiped the palm of her hand against the foggy window and looked out. She remembered last week when they had given Mr. Stamm a ride to church. Mr. Stamm was very old and lived alone. He could not see well enough to drive a car. Mr. Stamm had just seated himself next to Greg when Greg **blurted**, "You smell funny."

Yes, Greg had a problem with knowing when to speak and when not to speak, Meg thought. She turned from the window to watch Dad. He steered the van out of the parking lot and tried to think of a way to help Greg understand.

"Greg, you really must try harder to control yourself. A wise man thinks before he speaks."

"I was a Wise Man last Christmas," Greg said as he tugged and twisted his dented ping pong balls out of the ash tray. "I didn't speak because Mrs. Hansen said to put my gift down by Baby Jesus and keep my mouth shut."

Dad sighed and made a right turn onto Main Street.

Meg sat up straight and looked out of the window again. She knew that Main Street meant they were heading to Cassie's Drive-Up Donuts. She also knew the family rule, that if anyone asked for treats, Dad would not stop for any. He said we should all be thankful when something good came to us, but not beg. Of course, Meg saw that it was not good to whine or be greedy. But it could be awfully hard to get a treat with Greg in the car. If he looked up and saw Cassie's ahead, he would beg to get donuts and then they wouldn't get donuts after all.

Meg poked Seth, pointed to Greg, and put her finger to her lips. Seth leaned toward his brother and whispered, "OK, Greg, now is the time to think and not speak."

Greg looked up. He saw the donut shop ahead, and he saw Becca and Meg and Seth all looking at him with fingers to their lips and worry in their eyes.

"I know, I hafta keep my mouth quiet, or it is going to get in trouble," Greg whispered back to Seth.

Dad turned the van in at Cassie's and pulled up next to the drive-through window. He ordered a dozen maple bars and glazed donuts, and waited. Except for a soft gurgling sound, there was no noise from the back seat. Seth held his breath.

After what seemed like forever, a box of donuts was passed through the open car window into Dad's waiting hands. He was pleasantly surprised that Greg had not said a word.

Dad pulled back the cardboard lid and offered, "Would anyone like a donut?"

"Yes, please," Seth breathed again.

"Yes, please," said Meg.

"Yes, please," said Becca.

"Ahhh eeee uh iiiii aaaaa," said Greg.

"What in the world...?" Dad turned to the back seat. "Greg, what did you say, and *what* do you have in your mouth?"

Greg emptied his cheeks of the ping pong balls.

"I said, 'I'm being a wise man.'

"Please may I have a donut?"

"...he who restrains his lips is prudent." —*Prov. 10:19*

New Vocabulary

exited: left; went out the exit
blurted: spoke quickly, without thinking

Questions

1. What was the 'Peterson family rule'?
2. Dad said that we should all be thankful when _____.
3. What does a wise man do before he speaks?

It Seemed So Good

"Well, I don't know why your parents won't let you come to Sunday School with me. We're going to watch a movie at my church this week." Barbie rolled onto her stomach on the grassy creek bank and poked a stick into the water. A smoky cloud of mud rose from the creek bottom and flowed downstream.

"Well, movies are nice," Meg said, "but your church doesn't quite believe the same things that we do."

"Oh, what's the difference?" Barbie sat up and put her bare feet into the cool water. "You just do what the Bible says and do good stuff. You know, what feels right. That's all that really matters."

"Well, we do what the Bible says, too, but Dad says if you only do what you think feels right, you are deciding by feelings instead of by truth. If you really want to do what's right, you can't just pick and choose what you think the Bible means."

"Oh, that's so simple. You just read it and you know in your heart." Barbie made a face. "Anybody can tell what's good or bad."

"Anyway, what's this purple stuff?" Barbie leaned over and poked her face into the plastic bucket sitting next to her on the creek bank.

"Oh, that's just mashed blackberries and water," Meg said.

She stretched her arm past the bucket to the board that the girls used for a pretend stove. Meg moved the old, chipped cups, and picked up the cracked, wooden spoon that Mom had given her.

She slipped the spoon into the bucket and swirled it in big circles through the sparkling liquid.

"We were playing down here last weekend, but Becca and I never finished making our pretend blackberry soup. Doesn't it smell good?"

A sweet, fruity smell rose from the bucket. As Meg stirred, tiny bubbles rose to the top of the juice and popped.

"Mmmm." Barbie closed her eyes and sniffed. "I'm so thirsty that I could drink the whole bucket.

"Hey, why don't we have a tea party right here?" Barbie suggested. "You have those old dishes on your pretend stove, and we can drink the blackberry juice for 'tea.'"

Barbie picked up a mug with a broken handle and dipped into the purple juice.

Meg frowned. "I don't know, Barbie. It's just pretend soup, and Becca and I put some creek water in with the berries. Mom told us never to drink the creek water. It might make us sick."

"Oh, that's silly," said Barbie. "You use the creek water on your garden, don't you? And you eat vegetables from the garden and don't get sick." Barbie tossed her head and rolled her eyes at Meg.

"Anybody can tell it's OK."

She took a long drink from her cup.

"Just what I needed." Barbie smacked her lips and helped herself to another cupful.

Meg licked her dry lips and looked into the bucket. She was thirsty, too, and the berry soup smelled exactly like Mama's delicious blackberry cobbler. If Barbie thought the juice was good, it must be OK.

Meg filled a cup with the dark liquid and took a cautious sip of the purple 'tea.'

Why, it did seem to taste good after all! Meg tipped the cup back and thirstily drained it, leaving only a few seeds and berry skins stuck to the bottom of the mug...

Dear Reader, would you like to finish this story for me? How do you think it ended? Did you guess that Barbie's Mom called the Peterson home early the next morning, because Barbie had been horribly sick to her stomach all night? Did you figure out that Meg got sick at just the same time?

You probably already know that it isn't safe to drink water that isn't **sanitary**, or clean. And you know never to eat food that's been left out in the hot sun for a couple of days, even if your eyes tell you it looks good. That's because there are tiny germs, too small for our eyes to see, that are growing in the water and food. Those germs can make us very sick, just as they did Meg and Barbie.

But did you find another lesson in this story?

Barbie felt thirsty and the blackberry juice looked good. So Barbie let her feelings decide whether the juice was good or bad, instead of trying to find out if the juice was safe before she drank it.

Some people make choices about what is good or bad in God's eyes the same way. It they want to do something, why, it must be good! They don't turn to Jesus' Church to find out if there's something dangerous that they can't see, like 'spiritual germs' that could make their souls sick. Instead, they follow their feelings and end up in serious sin.

Thanks be to God that Jesus gave us His Church to guide us into all Truth. Instead of following our feelings, let's protect our souls from 'sickness' by following the teachings of Jesus' Church!

"In those days, there was no king in Israel; every man did what was right in his own eyes." —*Judg. 21:25*

"Do not be deceived: 'Bad company ruins good morals.'" —*I Cor. 15:33*

New Vocabulary

sanitary: clean and pure

Questions

1. "...Dad says if you only do what you think feels right, you are deciding by feelings instead of by _____."
2. Who can we trust to teach us the Truth?

For Discussion

Did Meg know that the creek water would make her sick? Why do you think she drank the juice anyway?

'My Special Time'

Dad leaned back in his recliner chair and shifted the newborn foster baby resting on his shoulder.

"Greg, stay there. Seth, can you straighten the burp rag under the baby's face for me?"

"Sure, Dad." Seth left his spot on the sofa to **adjust** the cloth. "Boy, he sure has little fingers, doesn't he? And look at those tiny fingernails!"

"I can fit his whole hand in my mouth," **boasted** Greg.

"Which is why you're still on the sofa and Seth is helping me now." Dad gave Greg a meaningful look.

Greg scooted over to take Seth's spot on the sofa and sighed a happy sigh. "I love babies. When I grow up, I'm gonna have a hunnerd babies and five kids."

Dad looked fondly at his dark-haired, dark-eyed boy and then at the **downy** blond head snuggled against his shoulder. "Yes, babies are wonderfully made, and truly a gift from the Lord."

"And he looks just like me," Greg noted.

"Truly," agreed Dad. "You both have beautiful souls and are made in God's image. Now, run see if the girls need a hand with the wash."

Mom had to meet with the baby's **caseworker** today, so Meg and Becca were helping with the extra wash. Babies sure did keep Mom busy!

Greg banged the dented laundry room door open against the battle-scarred washer and announced, "Daddy said I get to run the washing machine."

"I don't think so, but you can take the basket of clean diapers," Meg suggested. "Mom said you and Seth can fold them on the sofa."

Bumping through the doorway with the basket, Greg left the room. Meg filled the washing machine with pink and blue flannel sheets and baby blankets as Becca emptied the drier.

"I like these soft diapers." Becca pulled another warm cloth from the drier and rested her cheek in its fluffiness. "But I don't think I like that new faucet baby very much."

"You mean *foster* baby, but why don't you like him?" Meg was surprised. "He is so sweet!"

"'Cuz Mama was feeding the baby an' I asked if she would read me *The Treasure Box* story an' she said 'no,' an' she wouldn't listen to me. She told me I hafta wait for 'My Special Time.' "

Perhaps, dear Reader, I should explain 'My Special Time.' Each Tuesday and Thursday evening all of the children but one went to their rooms an hour before bedtime. There they could play quietly or snuggle into bed with a good book. The remaining child stayed up. He could pick whatever he wanted to do with Mom and Dad in that hour. Sometimes they read stories together. Sometimes they played checkers, or popped popcorn and sat on the porch and watched 'shooting stars.' One week the boys had 'My Special Time,' and the next week it was the girls' turn.

"Oh, Becca, this week is the boys' turn. Our time is next week."

"Well, I think maybe next week is tomorrow," Becca argued.

"No," Meg corrected patiently, "today's only Tuesday."

"But Tuesday is my turn! I want Mama to spend some time with me, not with that baby," Becca wailed.

"Look, Becca. Your turn is *next* Tuesday." Meg shut the washing machine and pushed in the knob. "I know it's hard to share Mama sometimes. But I know Someone who always, always has time for you. He's never too busy, and He's a good listener. Do you want to go spend some 'special time' with Him?"

If you could have followed the girls down the hall and into their room, this is what you would have seen: Meg took Becca to sit on her bed, in front of the little statue of the Infant of Prague on the shelf above. There, Becca told the Infant all about the 'other infant' who took so much of Mama's time.

And, when Becca had emptied her heart to the Holy Child, Meg read to her from *The Treasure Box*.

Dear Reader, do you know that Someone, who is never too busy for you?

"...the Lord hears when I call to him." —Ps.4:3

"For thou didst form my inward parts, thou didst knit me together in my mother's womb...Wonderful are thy works!"
—Ps. 139:13-14

New Vocabulary

adjust: to move something so it fits or works better
boasted: bragged
downy: like the soft under-feathers of a bird
caseworker: person who is in charge of cases; someone who makes sure the person they are responsible for is given good care

Questions

1. How did Meg and Becca help with the foster baby?
2. How did Seth and Greg help with the foster baby?
3. Becca was upset because Mama told her she had to wait for what?
4. How long do we have to wait if we want to spend time with Jesus?

 # Family Building Blocks

"Sit still, Greg, or you're going to lose an ear," ordered Mother. She was cutting the boys' hair and, as always, Greg was turning on the stool like the cat he'd once put into the clothes dryer.

"Meg, can you call Seth?" Mother asked. "I think he's outside, trying to fix Greg's dump truck."

"I wish I had a toy truck like the Uncles had when they were little," Greg said. "Grandad told me the sidewalk broke before the truck did." Greg hunched his neck down in the old sheet, trying to get away from the electric razor. "I wish I could call Grandad in Heaven so he could tell me the story about the truck again."

"Yes, Grandad had wonderful stories about growing up with the Uncles, didn't he?" Mother smiled.

"God is so good to give us families. Grandad Weathers grew up with nine brothers and two sisters. Haven't we been blessed that he and the

Uncles shared their happy memories and love and wisdom with us?"

Greg added a new nick to his haircut as he nodded, "But I want them to share the truck, too."

Seth, who was now washing his hands at the kitchen sink, remarked, "I can't get the wheels back on. Were you talking about Grandad's toy truck, the one that was made of **cast iron**? Grandad told me that was the only Christmas present he can remember that he got when he was a boy, and it wasn't just for him. All the Uncles shared it."

"That's the one present they got during the Depression, when nobody had any money," offered Meg. "Grandad said they wore the wheels off and then ran it on the sidewalk so much that it made little grooves in the concrete."

"I wish they made toys like that now," Seth said. "Although I did see a neat dump truck on TV at Nate's house."

Mom turned her head to one side as she brushed the hairs from Greg's neck and squinted at the haircut. Squinting made the haircut look better. It was too bad that everyone who looked at Greg wouldn't be squinting, thought Mom.

"Your turn, Seth."

"Hey, I didn't see any truck on EWTN." Greg hopped down from the stool. "Mama, can I turn the TV on?"

"No, Greg, you may not turn the TV on. The reason that you didn't see the toy **commercial** is because it's not on EWTN." Mom pinned the sheet around Seth's neck.

Seth started to ask why they couldn't watch other channels but decided to change his question. "Mom, I know that you call most TV programs 'junk for the soul,' but we could watch Catholic TV more, couldn't we? We don't even watch EWTN every day."

"I'm going to answer your question this way." Mother turned off the razor and reached for the scissors. "What is your favorite Weathers' story?"

"Oh, that's easy," Meg **interrupted**. "I like the story about when Uncle Wilbur was two and great-grandma heard him calling and she looked out the kitchen window and he had climbed to the very top of the windmill tower and was waving at her."

Out of the corner of his eye, Seth looked at Greg. "It's a good thing that we don't have a windmill.

"Windmill or not, my favorite story is when the Uncles were just teen-agers during the Depression, and they hopped a ride in a boxcar all the way from New Mexico to Oregon to look for work. They sure stuck together to help the family."

Greg rubbed his short hair vigorously, showering the floor with hair clippings. "My favorite story is about when they lived in New Hamster..."

"No, Greg, it was New *Mexico*."

for Little Folks Too

Greg ignored Seth and continued, "...and the Uncles were sleeping on the porch 'cuz it was too hot in the house and Uncle Kenny was little and he kept saying 'nake, nake' and finally the big boys woke up and there was a big, long, hugemungus rattlesnake all sleepy on the porch, too."

"Mom, those are all good stories." Seth blew a puff of air upward to free the loose, prickly hairs from his eyelashes. "But how do they answer my question about watching TV?"

Mom snipped across Seth's forehead as he closed his eyes. "Well, which story mentioned TV?"

Meg was truly puzzled. "None of them. Why?"

"I have one more question, first," said Mother. "What are some of your own favorite memories?"

"When we drove to Crater Lake and went camping and Becca and I sang 'Round and tasty on a bun; ketchup, onions, yum, yum, yum' over and over in the car all the way home and you and Daddy almost made us get out and walk," giggled Meg.

"Meg and us gave Butchie cat a bath and he looked so funny and then the bucket fell over and I got all wet and then I fell down and got a bloody nose and Meg picked me up and hugged me all the way to the house," Becca gave her big sister a happy squeeze.

"When we lay on the grass in the back yard and watched the falling stars streak through the pitch-black sky and heard the screech owls hunting mice in the field and Dad told us about watching the stars from the Navy ship when he was in Viet Nam. That's my favorite memory," said Seth.

"When Seth helped me learn how to ride his bike and I crashed into the picnic table and the spoke thingy got broken and he didn't get mad 'cuz I said 'sorry' and he said that's what brothers were for." Greg looked at his older brother with affection. "And next time, when you are little and I am big, I will help you learn how to ride a bike, too," Greg offered.

Seth felt the scissors stop and opened his eyes. "But this still doesn't answer my question about TV."

Mother turned the electric razor on again and began to trim the back of Seth's neck. "I think you have answered the question yourselves," remarked Mother.

"How many of the stories had a TV in them?"

"Do you see that memories come from times shared with each other, not time shared with TV?

"Our Lord, in His wisdom, created families to support one another, to help each other reach Heaven. All the Uncles' memories, and yours, are like building blocks for the family. Have you noticed that the Uncles are all good friends, and help each other out? Their building blocks, cemented together with love, are holding strong after all these years.

"Doing things together, reaching out to other people, those things are 'we centered,' and 'God centered.'

"TV is 'me centered.' It shuts people out. TV cannot give you a hug or teach you how to ride a bike or give you tissues for a bloody nose."

"And you can't sit on its lap," said Becca.

"That's right," continued Mother. "And God only gives us so many hours in each day. We need to use that time well, to reach out, not shut out."

"That's why you and Daddy won't let us use anything with earphones, either, isn't it?" Meg thought about her friend Barbie's CD player, and how hard it was to talk with her when Barbie was listening to music. "If you wear earphones, you can't hear anybody else. You're kind of in your own little world so you don't even notice other people."

"Exactly, Meg." Mother unpinned the sheet from around Seth's neck and handed it to him. "Go shake this outside while I sweep the floor.

"Greg and Meg, gather up the buckets by the woodpile. We are all going to help pick apples. When we finish, we'll come in, melt some caramel for the apples, and..."

"...and make some memories," finished Seth as he carried the hairy sheet through the door.

"Brothers and help are for a time of trouble..." —*Sir. 40:24*

New Vocabulary

cast iron: heavy type of metal
commercial: advertisement
interrupted: spoke out of turn

Questions

1. Why didn't Greg see the toy truck commercial on TV?
2. Mom said, "Doing things together, reaching out to other people, those things are _____."
3. "God only gives us so many hours in each day. We need to _____."

Tasting Temptation

Mother reached sleepily through the darkness for the bedside clock. It read 2:25 a.m.; yes, that would be the baby, waking for his feeding. As she replaced the alarm clock on the nightstand, Mother's hand paused in mid-air.

No, it couldn't have been the foster baby who had awakened her. Only yesterday, he had left for his forever home with his new mommy and daddy. Ah, I'm just too much in the habit of waking for his feeding, Mother thought as she turned over in bed.

She pulled the covers over her head, and prayed that God would bless the dear woman who loved and sacrificed to give her baby life. And how good God was, to answer the children's prayers for a loving Catholic family for 'faucet baby,' a family who would teach him to know, love, and serve Our Lord.

In **celebration**, she and the girls had baked a three-layer chocolate cake, buried in fudge frosting. Mother smiled **drowsily**. Ice cream and cake were probably dancing through the children's dreams. Well, the baby's adoption had been a wonderful thing to celebrate, and there was cake left over, waiting on the kitchen counter for tomorrow's snack. Mother drifted off to sleep to the peaceful sound of the ticking clock.

Mother was awake before the sunrise. For some reason, she hadn't slept well. I'll have to get used to life without a baby in the house, she thought as she headed down the dimly-lit hallway to the bathroom.

But what was that, littering the carpet outside the bathroom door and down the hall? It looked like a trail of Hansel and Gretel's bread crumbs! Mother bent for a closer look. No, it was bits of paper, and the trail led from the bathroom to Seth and Greg's room.

Mother switched on the bathroom light. Hmmm. Not just any paper, but bits of bandage wrappers; wrappers in the sink, wrappers on the floor. Now Mother could see that a trail of blood drops had joined the torn wrapper trail in its march across the bathroom floor toward the boys' room. Oh, dear. Hansel and Gretel must have had a serious accident.

Mother hurried to the boys' room and turned on their light. Seth squinted at the brightness and buried his head under the pillow. The bloody wrapper trail led right to Greg's bed and across his pillow, where a sleepy, frosting-covered face told the rest of the story.

"Greg! Wake up!" Mother checked quickly to see that Greg, under the chocolate, still had most of his fingers. "Take those bandages off, now!"

Greg blinked sleepily and sat up. "Mommy, I didn't want to eat the cake."

"Funny, Greg," Mother said as she fearfully examined her sticky son, "but I didn't say anything about cake. After I look at your fingers, we are going to visit the kitchen together."

"But, Mommy," **protested** Greg, "I didn't *want* to eat the cake."

"Greg, you are not being honest. And you have a pretty bad cut on your finger, but I don't think this one will need stitches. Get up," Mother said **grimly**. "We're going to the kitchen."

A short march down the hall brought mother and son to the kitchen. There, on the counter, in the middle of a chocolate-frosting finger-painting, sat an empty cake plate. That is, it would have been empty, if the biggest knife in the kitchen had not been resting across it.

"Greg!" Mother shrieked. "You know you aren't supposed to touch the knives! I don't even know how you managed to reach them!"

"It's easy, but you hafta stand on the counter."

"And why did you have to use the biggest knife in the kitchen to cut the cake?" Mother asked tiredly.

"'Cuz it was the biggest *cake* in the kitchen," Greg answered. "Anyway, I wouldn't have got a cut, but I didn't want to turn the light on and wake you up. I'm sorry, Mommy." Greg hung his head.

"You mean that you did this all in the dark?" Mother dropped down onto the stool. Now she knew why she had awakened during the night. "Greg, you could have hurt yourself very badly. By taking the cake, you were stealing and being disobedient. And then you did not tell the truth when you said that you didn't eat it. Do you see that once you started to sin, the sin got worse and worse?

"The next time you are **tempted** to do something bad, stop and think first. Ask Jesus for help, and then grab your Guardian Angel's hand and run away from the temptation."

"But I didn't *want* to eat the cake, Mommy. You know how you always say if we don't want to eat something at dinner, we don't need to eat it all, but we need at least to take a little taste?

"Well, I didn't *want* to eat the cake, so I just took lots of little tastes and all of a sudden the cake wasn't there anymore."

Dear Reader, do you ever take a 'taste' of temptation? It's a very dangerous thing to do, you know, as Greg found out. The Church, in her wisdom, teaches us to avoid the 'near occasion of sin' and not to 'entertain' sinful thoughts. If we don't 'taste' the temptation in our minds, we won't be tempted to fall into sin. Better yet, let us 'taste and see the goodness of the Lord!'

"...for you have tasted the kindness of the Lord. Come to him..."
—1 Pet. 2:3 & 4

"For because he himself has suffered and been tempted, he is able to help those who are tempted." —Heb. 2:18

New Vocabulary

celebration: have a party to mark a special occasion
drowsily: sleepily
protested: objected or denied
grimly: more than seriously
tempted: wanting to do something sinful

Questions

1. How did Mother know that Greg had eaten the cake, even before she went into the kitchen?
2. Mother said, "Do you see that once you started to sin, _____?"
3. Who can help us when we are tempted to sin?

Whining Mosquitos

Mother entered the kitchen just in time to see the top of a head and a pair of eyes, barely **visible** above the counter. The eyes stared at a plate of crisp peanut butter cookies, hot from the oven, sitting in the center of the counter.

From the same side of the counter, a small hand crept toward the plate of cookies, just as Mother lifted the plate to a safe place on top of the refrigerator.

The head, eyes, and hand belonged to Harley's five-year-old brother, David. [Do you remember meeting Seth's friend Harley in the first book of *Devotional Stories for Little Folks?*]

"Are those peanut butter cookies?" David asked. "I like to be baby-sat at your house. Can I have a cookie?"

"Yes," Mother answered, "you may have a cookie at snack time later this afternoon."

"But I wanna cookie *nowwww*." David plopped to the floor in a heap, like a balloon that suddenly has lost all its air. "I *neeeeed a cookieeeeeee*," David whined from the kitchen floor.

Without answering, Mother turned toward the dining room, leaving the kitchen and David behind.

"Good! You've cleared the table already," Mother said as she handed an old bedsheet to Meg.

"Here is the cover for your covered wagon."

"Whoa, there!" Seth pulled back hard on the jump-rope 'reins' tied to Becca's rocking horse. He slid off the wooden bench set up in front of the table, and reached for a corner of the sheet.

"Let me help you get that top up before the storm starts. See those big black clouds in the distance?" Seth waved his hand at the bare dining room wall as he helped Meg drape the bedsheet over the table.

David's grumpy face appeared in the dining room doorway.

"I wanna watch cartoons."

"We don't watch cartoons," Mother said. She lifted one side of the old sheet so that David could see Meg and Becca underneath the table, tying sunbonnets on their dolls.

"Would you like to play in the covered wagon?"

"I wanna watch *cartooooooooons*," David whined in a high voice. "I always watch cartoons at my house."

"Do you hear a mosquito?" Meg giggled to Seth from inside the 'covered wagon.'

"Yup, they seem to be real bad in these parts. Kinda whiny and real annoying." Seth slapped at **imaginary** insects as he looked over his shoulder at David. "Funny how those mosquitos always drive Mom away.

"Hey, David, come ride up here with me," Seth offered, patting the bench beside him.

"No," pouted David, "I wanna go outside and ride your bike. I wanna ride the *biiiiiike*, I said!" David looked to see if Mother had heard him, but she had left when David started to whine again.

"One thing you should know about my mom," Seth said, "is that she can't hear you when you whine. If you want something, you need to ask her in a normal voice, or she'll never hear you, and she won't ever, ever, answer you."

"Well, how come I can't ride your bike?" David mumbled. "It's not fair."

"You know the bike is too big for you," Seth explained. "The last time you were here, it fell over on top of you because you couldn't reach the pedals and you got all banged up. Besides, it's cold and rainy outside. Why don't you play with us?"

David pouted, stamped his foot, and repeated, "No! It's just not *fair*!"

Meg, on her hands and knees under the table, stuck her head out from under the worn sheet so that it draped like a shawl over her head and shoulders.

for Little Folks Too

"Why do you want to do something that will hurt you? Besides, the whole time you've been whining and pouting, we've been doing something fun! Instead of wasting your time being unhappy about something that you can't do, why not be happy doing something that you can do?"

"Yeah," added Seth, "and instead of feeling sorry for yourself about things you can't have, thank God for the good things you do have."

"Father Dominic says that, because all God's ways are good, even 'bad' things turn out to have something good hidden inside." Meg pointed to the window and the gray drizzle outside. "Because it rained, we got to play 'covered wagon.'"

David's pout slowly disappeared as he climbed onto the bench next to Seth. "You mean like 'cuz I can't ride your bike, I won't skin my knees?"

"Yup!" Seth handed the jump-rope 'reins' to David. "So instead, you get to lead the whole wagon train over the Rocky Mountains. Now, tell that horse to giddy-up!"

Dear Reader, when you are tempted to look only at the 'bad' side of things, trust in God's goodness. Thank Him for the situation and see if you can find something good hidden inside.

"...give thanks in all circumstances; for this is the will of God in Christ Jesus for you." —*1 Thess. 5:18*

"Be happy and at peace. Accept whatever [God] gives, and give whatever He takes, with a big smile." —Bl. Teresa of Calcutta

New Vocabulary

visible: able to be seen
imaginary: not real; pretend

Questions

1. What did David want to do outside?
2. What had happened to David when he had tried to ride Seth's bike before?
3. Meg said, "Instead of wasting your time being unhappy about something that you can't do, _____."

God's Wise Order

"Becca, it's time to put your dolls away and get ready for bed."

"But, Mama," Becca protested in a whiny voice, "Curly Locks is getting ready for bed, too, and I need to wash her face first. I hafta go get a washcloth, and then I need to change her diaper."

"No, Becca, playtime is done. It's time to put the toys away."

"But I hafta get a washcloth, *now*!" Becca argued as she snatched up Curly Locks and stomped toward the bathroom.

"Becca, I don't know what's gotten into you!" Mother was shocked. "You are usually my good, obedient girl.

"Hmmmm..." Mother tried to think. "Maybe you're coming down with a bad case of *daviditis*."

"Oh, no, Mommy," Becca stopped, suddenly worried. "What is *davi-doofus*?" She put one hand

46   *Devotional Stories*

on her forehead and one on her tummy. "Am I gonna be sick?"

"Well," Mother said as she reached for Becca's shoulder and marched her to the time-out stool, "all I can tell you right now is that this is the best cure."

Becca suddenly felt very hot and shaky. She wanted to ask more about her strange illness, but she knew that it was not smart to talk while she was in time-out. Talking in time-out meant even more time on the stool. Besides, Mama would not answer her while she was in time-out, anyway.

After several minutes, the kitchen timer rang, telling Becca that she could get up and say 'sorry' to Mama. Becca knew that she would not be able to wash Curly Lock's face or change her diaper now. Curly Locks would be gone, because talking back meant losing whatever you were playing with when you talked back, period. It was time for bed, anyway. Becca sighed and walked slowly to the kitchen to find Mama.

"Mommy," Becca hugged Mama's legs, "I'm sorry that I talked back and didn't do what you told me to do. Am I going to be sick in the night? Can I take a big bowl to bed? What is *davi-doofus*?"

"I forgive you, honey. It's past time for bed now, but I will you tell you about *daviditis* in the morning." Mother's half-smile tried to say something that her words didn't. "I don't think you'll be sick in the night. Now, run brush your teeth and get your jammies on, and we'll say prayers together."

The next morning, Mother was in the kitchen, stirring a pot of bubbling oatmeal and raisins when Becca stumbled in.

She rubbed the sleep from her eyes with her small fists. "Mama, I had a bad dream." Becca buried her face in Mother's skirt.

"Oh, dear, honey." Mother moved the pot off the burner and knelt down to hug Becca. "Can you tell me what the dream was about?"

"Yes, Mommy," Becca sniffed, "I dreamed you were talking back to me."

Mother's half-smile returned. "Yes, you definitely have all the **symptoms** of *daviditis*. I guess breakfast can wait a few minutes while I explain.

"You see, honey, every time David comes over to play, he always seems to leave little germs behind. He goes home, but he leaves some of his **behavior** germs with you. Then my good little girl starts to talk back, and whine, and disobey. She has a case of *daviditis*!"

"Well, I don't like sitting on that stool, Mommy, and I don't like that *davi-doofus*. Can you call David's mommy and tell her that he has to do time-out for me next time, 'cuz he's the one who made me sick?"

"I'm afraid it doesn't work that way, honey. You are responsible for your behavior, and David is responsible for his behavior.

"You see," Mother went on, "David's parents are nice people, but they aren't Catholic. They don't know that, when God gives parents the wonderful gift of children, He also gives them His **authority** to raise the children. All children belong to Him, you know.

"God made parents older, bigger, stronger, and wiser..."

"And," interrupted Becca, "sometimes bald."

"Yes, sometimes bald," agreed Mother, "so they could raise their children well. But most important of all, God gives special graces to parents, through the Sacrament of Matrimony, to know what is best for children. From God, to Daddy and Mama, to you. All in God's wise order."

"For the Lord honored the father above the children, and he confirmed the right of the mother over her sons." —*Sir. 3:2*

"For there is no authority except from God, and those that exist have been instituted by God. Therefore he who resists the authorities resists what God has appointed..." —*Rom. 13:1-2*

New Vocabulary

symptoms: signs of an illness
behavior: how a person acts
authority: a right to lead, to be the one in charge

Questions

1. Why was Becca suddenly being naughty?
2. Which sacrament gives graces especially for raising children?
3. To whom does God give those graces?

Created for My Glory

Seth, Meg, and Becca sat, elbows on the kitchen counter, nibbling their oatmeal chocolate chip cookie snack.

Greg was also at the counter, but working on his math paper. He looked at the cookie-eaters around him and announced cheerfully, "Mommy said when I ate the cake that I had enough dessert for a week. I am having a math paper and 'sorry sentences' today, but I will have a cookie tomorrow."

"Here, Seth." Greg pushed a pile of wrinkled papers and his small, red race car toward Seth. "I finished my 'sorry sentences' to you, and here is my car, too. I'm sorry I broke your train tracks. They went up and down in Becca's toy toaster just like real toast, until they had to go and break.

"I hope you like the car. It goes fast when it has wheels."

"Thanks, Greg." Seth took the crumpled papers and battered car. "Maybe I can find some new wheels for it and we can race cars together when you finish your math paper."

Forty-five minutes later, Greg was still at the kitchen counter, bent over his addition problems. He twisted back and forth on the stool, trying to remember those flash cards. Did two plus four equal seven, or was it eight?

Meanwhile, Seth was sweating and grunting as he tried to do jumping jacks in the living room, only a few feet from where Greg was puzzling over his now-wrinkled and well-erased paper.

Snap! Greg's pencil lead, pressed hard against his paper, broke into little pieces.

Greg hopped down from the stool, looking **longingly** at Seth as he skipped by on the way to the pencil sharpener. How he wished that he could trade places with Seth. Greg was really good at jumping jacks!

As he tried to make his arms and legs come together at the same time, Seth could hear the sharpener, grinding away at Greg's pencil. Seth looked longingly at his brother as Greg returned to the stool, carrying his pencil stub. How Seth wished he could trade places with Greg. Seth was really good at math!

Greg slowly climbed onto his stool to see that only six problems were done on one side. He turned the paper over. Nope, no more problems on that side. Good!

But look! He could see through the holes! Greg put the math paper over his face, and turned to look at Seth through the holes he had erased in the paper.

"Hey, Seth! I can see you! Your arms and legs are doing a dance."

"Yeah, I know. But your holey paper looks pretty funny, too. I bet I could finish your addition problems in thirty seconds flat, and you could do perfect jumping jacks in your sleep. Doesn't seem fair, does it?"

"Hey, Seth!" Greg was down from the stool in a flash and at Seth's side. "We can trade places. I can be you and you can be me. I will do your jumping jacks for you, and you can do my paper.

"I will do jumping jacks and cartwheels for you, like this." Arms and legs flying, Greg was already cartwheeling circles down the Peterson's long, wide hallway.

"Boy, Greg, you sure can do cartwheels," admired Seth. "I bet you could even do them with one hand."

Greg immediately set about showing Seth that he could, indeed, cartwheel with one hand.

"Wow, Greg." Seth was even more admiring. Without thinking, he blurted, "Can you do cartwheels with no hands, too?"

Unfortunately, Greg was sure that he could, and there was nothing that he wouldn't try.

He pulled himself up to a sitting position on the hallway floor, rubbed the back of his neck, and shared his discovery. "No, Seth. I can't do cartwheels with no hands. Ouch."

"I'm sorry, Greg." Seth helped Greg up off the floor. "C'mon, I'll help you with your addition. I'll get out the counting cubes so you can see how many to add.

"Anyway, it would be pretty funny if we traded places with each other." Seth chuckled as the boys reached the kitchen counter, arm in arm. "If we traded places, then I would be **talented** at jumping jacks and cartwheels, but I couldn't do math at all.

"You would be talented at math, but not cartwheels and jumping jacks. So we wouldn't really be any better off than we were before.

"Besides, I think it's neat that you are so strong." Seth felt the arm muscle that Greg proudly offered.

"And you are the hardest worker I know. You never give up, and you are always cheerful. I'm glad God made you just the way you are."

Dear Reader, wouldn't it seem odd if a bowl of ice cream wished it were a shoe, or a shoe wished that it were a bowl of ice cream? What if each tried to do the other's job? Ice cream is delicious, and it has its place. Shoes keep our feet warm and safe; they have a job to do, too. But I don't think you'd like your ice cream on your feet, nor your shoes in a sugar cone.

God made each of us for a special purpose in life. *No one else* can ever do the job that God made us for, if we will do our best with the talents that God gave to us. He made us for His glory, and He loves us, for He is our Creator!

When Seth and Greg were grown, they both did fine jobs of using the talents that God had given to them. Would you be surprised to learn that, when Seth grew up, he became a **professor**? And Greg got a job breaking things.

His boss at the recycling center said Greg was his best worker. He could crush cans and bottles faster than anyone the boss had ever hired.

"...everyone who is called by my name, whom I created for my glory, whom I formed and made." —Is. 43:7

"...you are precious in my eyes, and honored, and I love you..." —Is. 43:4

New Vocabulary

longingly: with wishful desire; wistfully
talented: able to do a thing especially well
professor: teacher

Questions

1. What toy did Greg give to Seth? Why do you think he gave his toy to Seth?
2. Who gave Seth the talent to be good at math?
3. Who gave Greg the talent to be good at jumping jacks?

For Discussion

Why should we be thankful for the talents that we have?

Why should we work to get better at the things we are good at?

Living Examples

In her fuzzy yellow ducky jammies, Becca stood with stretched tiptoes on the little wooden stool at the bathroom sink. She was scrubbing her teeth for bedtime, just minutes away.

Behind Becca, Meg was making monster faces in the mirror as she waited her turn at toothbrushing. With the fingers of her left hand, she pulled her lower eyelids down. With her right hand, Meg pushed the end of her nose up, to make a pig's snout. Then she stuck her tongue down, down almost to her chin.

Becca, her mouth foamy with toothpaste, choked with laughter at Meg's face in the mirror.

"Meg, you are a Monster Pig." Becca dropped her toothbrush on the counter and pulled the corners of her mouth into a wide frown. She stuck out a foamy tongue.

"And I am Monster Clown." Becca laughed through stretched lips as Mother brought an armful of newly folded towels into the bathroom.

"Bedtime, girls."

Soon, Becca and Meg were headed for bed, giggling over their funny faces.

The next morning, while they dressed, Meg made a pig snout and wagged her head back and forth, back and forth, at Becca.

After lunch, as Mother cleared the dishes and Meg wiped the table, Becca made a pig snout and pulled her eyelids down, wagging her head and giggling at Meg.

That afternoon, the girls were doing their schoolwork at the table. Meg was working on a page in her Language book. She found and circled the nouns, while Becca took out four new *Little Stories for Little Folks'* flashcards to color.

Becca was using her new BerrySmelly Colors; should she use BlackBerry, BerryRose, or GrapeBerry?

Today, most of the flashcards would be purple, Becca decided, because the purple color smelled like grape bubble gum balls.

Meg watched as Becca's scribbling hand buried the flashcard in a thick coat of purple wax. She knew that, ever since Greg peeled the paper labels off all the colors, Becca did not like to share them with anyone. But Meg still wished that she could use the rose color. Rose was one of her favorite **fragrances**. Besides, the pink would look pretty in the Language book.

"Becca, please may I use one of your colors?" Meg asked sweetly.

Becca did not say anything, but answered Meg with a monster face.

"Mom, Becca's making faces at me!" Meg called in a hurt voice.

Mother stuck her head through the doorway. "Why, Meg, I don't understand why you are upset. You are a good teacher."

"I'm a good teacher?" Meg pointed her pencil at Becca. "But she is making ugly faces at me."

"That's right," Mother pointed out, "she is making the faces that you taught her. If you don't like the way Becca copies you, maybe you need to find something nicer for her to copy.

"You know that Becca looks up to you, as her big sister," Mom went on. "Being an older sister is a big responsibility, because you set an example for the children who are younger.

"Think of the saints. Their lives are good examples for us to **imitate**, aren't they?"

Meg twisted one of her dark braids around her finger, and thought about the story they'd been reading about St. Therese. Her older sisters had been like 'other mothers' to St. Therese when she was small. They had helped the little girl, who would become a great saint, learn how to share by their example.

"Like St. Therese!" Meg told Mother. "I can try to imitate her, and her older sisters."

"Good." Mom gave Meg's shoulder a friendly squeeze. "That's the way. We can imitate the saints, just as they imitated Jesus. They set an example for us. And now it's our turn to be living examples of Christ, to our families and to the world."

All afternoon, Meg thought about good examples and bad examples. She thought about the kindness and mercy that Jesus showed to the world, even to those who didn't love Him back.

Meg decided that, each day, she would try to set a good example for Becca. She would think of some kindness to do, even if Becca did nothing for her.

That evening, Meg let a surprised Becca play with her favorite tea set, before Becca even asked.

The next day, when Becca was having trouble making the back yard swing 'go,' Meg pushed her high in the air. Then she patiently showed Becca how to pump her short legs back and forth, back and forth, to make the swing go higher all by herself.

A few days passed, and Meg and Becca were back at the table with their schoolwork. With a plain black marker, Meg was tracing a map of Canada. Across the table, Becca had four more flashcards to color. She had decided that today would be a cherry day, so today's flashcards would be red.

Back and forth, back and forth, the CherryBerry color spread across the thin cardboard square. Becca put her nose to the flashcard and sniffed the **delicious**, sweet cherry fragrance. She looked up at Meg, who was carefully printing city names on her map. Becca looked down at her box of colors.

"Here, Meggy. I am just coloring with cherries today, not roses. If you want, you can use my smelly colors."

"...be imitators of God, as beloved children. And walk in love, as Christ loved us and gave himself up for us..."   —*Eph. 5:1 & 2*

New Vocabulary

fragrances: pleasant odors
imitate: copy
delicious: tasty

Questions

1. Mom said, "Being an older sister is a big responsibility because _____."
2. What two things did Meg do for Becca to set a good example?
3. In the end, how did Becca copy Meg's good example?

A Log Truck for Jesus

Under the sheltering maple tree in the cows' pasture, inside the 'Fatima Clubhouse' that the children themselves had built the summer before, Seth, Greg, and Seth's friend, Nate Blake, were meeting.

"In the Name of the Father, and of the Son, and of the Holy Spirit, Amen."

The boys finished praying the decade that always opened their meetings and Seth got right to the reason he had called the boys together.

"Advent just started, and Christmas will be here in a couple of weeks. I've been trying to think of something nice we can do for Jesus, since it's His birthday."

"Yeah," Nate nodded, "every time we go to the store, it's all about presents we can buy for everybody but Him. It seems like people forget whose birthday it really is. There are things a lot more important than just getting more 'stuff.'

"Father Dominic said Jesus is here with us," Nate went on, "in 'the least of these,' so we could do some kind of Corporal Work of Mercy for Jesus. But what can we give Him?"

Greg **solemnly** shook his head from side to side. "Don't give Him any hay. I tried to give Him some for His manger, but He didn't want it."

"He didn't want it?" puzzled Nate.

"Yeah, every time I threw it up to Heaven, Jesus threw it back at me, and it got in my eyes."

Nate leaned back on the rough boards of the clubhouse wall and burst into laughter. "Oh, Greg, you are too funny. Jesus didn't throw hay at you. That was **gravity**."

"No, Nate, it wasn't gravity, it was *hay*," Greg answered earnestly.

"What Nate means, Greg, is what we were talking about at morning devotions today," explained Seth. "Remember that verse about Jesus being named Emmanuel? Emmanuel means 'God *with* us.' Jesus isn't just in Heaven, but right here. So if we do something kind for somebody, it is just like doing it for Jesus. That's how we give gifts to Him."

The distant sound of a heavy truck, shifting down to climb a steep logging road, drifted over the forested hills and into Greg's bouncing thoughts.

"Hey, we could get Him a truck!"

Seth rolled his eyes, but Nate cried, "That's it!"

Seth couldn't believe what he was hearing. "You're kidding, right?" Nate never agreed with Greg. "Where would we get the money to buy Jesus a log truck, and what in the world would He do with it?"

"No, not a truck, but trees. Wood! Firewood! Today they finish logging on the hill behind our house. The timber company always leaves some fallen trees for other people to use, and I'll bet we can get our dads to cut some up for old Grandma Potts. She doesn't have any money to pay for heating her house, but she has a wood stove. I know, because I've seen the smoke from her chimney. And she's too old to cut firewood herself."

"Hey, yeah! And Mrs. Barton, at the other end of the road. She's a widow, and could use some wood, too. Free firewood would save them money and keep them warm this winter."

Later that evening, Nate told his father about their idea, while Seth and Greg had almost the same conversation at their house.

"...so, if you can cut the wood, we can help load it and stack it at Grandma Potts' house, and at Mrs. Barton's, too," finished Seth.

"I can help, too, Daddy," Greg said. "You can axe it, and I can chainsaw."

Dad shuddered at the thought of the words 'chainsaw' and 'Greg' being together even in the same sentence, let alone in person.

"No, Greg, you're not big enough yet. We'll cut the wood and then pick you up when we are done. You can come with us to the ladies' houses and help unload. I'll call Nate's dad and see how this Saturday sounds.

"I'm proud of you boys, that you have thought of this gift for Jesus. Our Lord shows us how to give, by giving us the greatest Gift ever. Jesus asked nothing for Himself, but gave us His all. I think you understand what Christmas is about. It's not what we *get*, but what we *give*."

That Saturday afternoon, Dad used his chainsaw to cut the fallen logs, lying scattered on the hillside. Mr. Blake split the cut pieces into firewood while the boys watched from a safe distance.

Seth and Nate then carried the heavy chunks of wood to the pickup truck. Staggering and grunting, the boys pushed them onto the pickup bed. Piece by piece, the truck began to fill.

When the truck was nearly overflowing with firewood, the cutting and splitting and carrying was done. It was time to drive home to get Greg, and then make their first delivery.

Now the boys would move the wood a second time, this time unloading all that they had piled in the truck a short time before.

For the next few hours, first Grandma Potts and then Mrs. Barton watched with grateful eyes as Nate, Seth, and Greg strained their muscles to carry and stack the 'Christmas firewood' in neat rows next to their houses. Finally, the last piece of firewood was set in place.

Brushing bits of bark and mud from the front of their jackets and jeans, Seth and Greg waved a final 'good-bye' to Mrs. Barton and climbed into the front seat of the truck. Although their muscles were complaining, the boys began the drive home with happy hearts.

"It's funny, Dad," smiled Seth as he picked slivers from his red, chapped hands, "but I almost feel like I'm the one that got the Christmas gift."

"Yeah, those ladies thanked me lots and told me I was a big boy," **beamed** Greg.

"Now that I'm big, can I have a chainsaw for Christmas?"

"'Behold, a virgin shall conceive and bear a son, and his name shall be called Emmanuel' (which means, God with us).'"
—Matt. 1:23

"'Truly, I say to you, as you did it to one of the least of these my brethren, you did it to me.'" —Matt. 25:40

New Vocabulary

solemnly: seriously
gravity: scientific force that makes what goes up, come down
beamed: smiled a bright smile

Questions

1. What does 'Emmanuel' mean?

2. By helping Grandma Potts and Mrs. Barton, who were the boys really 'helping'?
3. Dad said, "I think you understand what Christmas is about. It's not what we get, but what we _____."

Something to Do

Make a sign listing the Corporal Works of Mercy. See how many of the Works you can do this month, or during Advent.

Mending More than a Top

It had been his favorite spinning top, with the red and blue and silver race cars on the side that got all blurry when you pulled the string, until the string broke off and then all those little pieces of rope that he cut wouldn't fit the hole for the string and the hammer and screwdriver somehow made the top into lots of pieces that didn't fit together anymore.

Greg pulled on his ears to make them listen to Daddy again.

"...you must understand that there are **consequences** to your actions. What you do affects not only you, but can hurt others as well. So you must learn to think before you act, and be honest enough to tell on yourself. Sins can't be fixed until they are confessed.

"So you may not go into the workshop for two weeks, even if I am working there. And no more rope, without asking me first. Is that clear?"

"Yes, Daddy," sniffed Greg from the time-out stool. It would be hard not to be in the workshop watching and helping Daddy. How would Daddy manage without him? Daddy said that everything he'd ever learned about fixing and mending things, he'd learned from Greg.

"I'm sorry I cut your rope up and then hid it so you wouldn't find out. I won't play with the rope in the workshop any more."

"OK, then. Now, say your Act of Contrition, and you can go play."

"O my God, I am hardly sorry for having offended Thee. I 'test all my sins 'cuz I fear my just punishments, but most of all because they offend Thee, my God, Who are all-good and deserving of all my love. I firmly resolve, with the help of Thy grace, to confess my sins, to do menace, and 'mend my life. Amen."

"And remind me," Dad gave Greg a friendly pat on the back, "to help you practice your Act of Contrition tonight at bedtime."

Freed from the stool, Greg headed outside to play with his beloved guinea pig, Jack. It was not fun to have to sit in one place on the time-out stool, Greg thought. Jack must get pretty bored staying in one place all the time, too.

I will go get Jack and let him run around a bit, Greg decided. Greg often played with Jack in the back of Dad's pickup. It was like having a fenced yard just for boys and guinea pigs, with no chance that Jack would get loose.

Greg opened the heavy wire lid of Jack's cage. Jack whistled a guinea pig greeting as Greg lifted him from his safe, cozy home.

Hugging the little brown ball of fur in his arms, Greg headed for the pickup. He skipped, hopped, and turned in circles as he made his way to the truck. Going in circles was fun, because it made the trees dance funny as they whirled around you.

If you went in circles long enough, you got dizzy and then fell over, just like my top, thought Greg. Boy, mending broken stuff was harder than it looked. And then Dad said he couldn't get another top until next year because of that consequence stuff.

Hey, maybe I could make a top, Greg thought. I would just need something that would spin and a string to wrap around it and pull!

Or something like string. Right there, hanging on the pegboard in the garage, was some skinny rope.

Uh-oh. Dad said no rope without asking.

But it looks more like **cord** than rope, Greg told himself. Using the cord would not be breaking his promise not to use rope, would it? And he wouldn't cut it this time, so nothing would get hurt.

Greg shifted Jack under one arm and reached for the thin rope with the other. He tossed the rope into the pickup bed, and then dropped Jack onto the cool, metal floor. As Greg climbed over the tailgate to join Jack, his brain was buzzing with ideas for his new top.

I just need something that I can wrap the cord around, something that can spin, thought Greg. He watched Jack stretching his legs as he peacefully explored the pickup bed.

Wait! Couldn't Jack spin? Jack's beady black eyes looked trustingly at Greg as he was scooped up against Greg's T-shirt. Greg began to turn in tight circles, growing dizzier and dizzier as the garage whirled around him in a blur. See? He and Jack were spinning around right now!

Greg stopped, even though his eyes were still going in circles. He waited for the truck floor to quit moving. Then Greg picked up the rough rope and began to wrap it around and around Jack's furry brown body. The rope wound around Jack's back legs, then his tummy, then his front legs. Jack was beginning to look like a mummy.

At last, only Jack the Top's trusting beady eyes showed above the coils of rope.

Greg set Jack on the metal pickup bed. With one hand, he held Jack upright. With the other hand, Greg held the rope's end.

Just then, Jack decided that he did not like being a mummy. He did not like being a top. He would chew his way to freedom. Jack sank his long front teeth deep into the rope.

Poor Jack. At that moment, Greg gave a mighty pull to the end of the rope.

When Jack stopped spinning, he was free of the rope. Unfortunately, he was also free of his front teeth.

Poor, poor Jack. Because Greg didn't think about consequences before he made Jack into a top, Jack's front teeth had broken off right at the gumline. It would be very hard for him to eat for a few weeks.

Dear Reader, I must tell you here that our good Creator gave all **rodents**, including guinea pigs, special teeth. Rodents **gnaw**, or chew, all the time, which makes their teeth wear out quickly. Because of this gnawing, God gave them teeth that always keep growing. Jack's teeth soon grew back, but he certainly had a hard time eating until they did.

And poor Greg. If only he had stopped himself when he was tempted to take the rope! Now, he would have to tell Daddy about Jack, and about the rope, too.

Greg sighed. He wished he could go to Confession, like Seth and Meg. Seth said Confession took your sins away, and then mended your soul so it was like new. And it made big muscles in your soul, too, so you could be stronger against sin the next time.

"Jesus, please help me do what's right," Greg prayed as he carefully tucked Jack inside his shirt. "I hafta go tell Daddy, but I sure don't want to. Please help me 'mend my life, and help Daddy fix Jack. Amen."

Greg, head down, turned toward the house, dragging his feet so his black rubber boots made long tracks in the grass. Slowly, he turned the knob on the back door. He shook his boots off so they landed close to the boot shelf, if not quite on the shelf itself. Even more slowly, he crept into the living room.

Dad heard the soft swish of Greg's dragging footsteps on carpet.

"Daddy?"

"Yes, Greg?" Dad set the newspaper he was reading in his lap and waited.

Greg nervously patted the furry bulge, wiggling under his T-shirt.

"Remember one time when we went to old Mr. Stamm's house and when he opened the door he didn't have his false teeth in, and his mouth looked kind of puckery?

"Well, Daddy, did you ever notice how much Jack looks like Mr. Stamm?"

"He who conceals his transgressions will not prosper, but he who confesses and forsakes them will obtain mercy."   —*Prov. 28:13*

New Vocabulary

consequences: good or bad results of our actions
cord: thin rope
rodents: rats, mice, squirrels, guinea pigs
gnaw: chew

Questions

1. Dad said, "...there are **consequences** to your actions. What you do _____."
2. What do you think Greg should have done when he was tempted to take the rope?
3. How did Jack lose his teeth?
4. Can you correct Greg's Act of Contrition?

With thanks to the David Born family, for an 'inspirational' Act of Contrition.

Much More than a Tree

Greg watched as Dad's electric drill whined, growled, and chewed a hole through the piece of pine on the workshop bench.

The growling stopped, as Dad set the tool aside to brush sawdust from the hole.

"Here you go, Greg." Dad handed the flat, wooden crown to Greg. "Do you think this will fit on our Jesse tree?"

"Yes, Daddy. Can I have an electric drill for Christmas?"

"Sure, when you are forty-five. Now, how about taking these ornaments into the house? I think Meg and Seth are waiting to paint them."

In the family room, Meg's friend Barbie fingered the rich softness of the purple **velvet** cloth under the bare, dry branches of the Jesse tree.

"This fabric is nice, but that's the weirdest Christmas tree I've ever seen. How come you

Devotional Stories

guys don't have a real Christmas tree? We've had our tree up since Thanksgiving."

"That's not a Christmas tree; it's a Jesse tree," Meg giggled. "It's not time for a Christmas tree yet."

"Don't you have a Jesse tree at your house?" Seth asked. He moved the evergreen Advent wreath to one side and spread newspapers over the dining table. "Here comes Greg with the ornaments. You can help paint them, if you want."

Barbie pulled out a chair and reached for one of the water color paint sets, as Greg scattered wooden ornaments across the newspapers. With her paintbrush, she pointed to the Advent wreath.

"How come you put your wreath on the table, instead of on the door, and where are your presents?"

"Well," Seth began, "there's a lot more to Christmas than presents and a Christmas tree.

"In our house, we start with the Advent wreath. Every night, we gather around it and sing 'O Come, O Come, Emmanuel.' We read a verse and then we light the pink and purple candles. The candles shine in the darkness, reminding us of the Light to come."

Greg held high his dripping paintbrush, like a candle melting over his head.

"And Daddy gives everybody twinkly electric candles to put in our bedroom windows, so we can't burn the house down."

Seth ran the bristles of his damp brush over the yellow paint square as he continued.

"A few days after Advent begins, we start hanging ornaments on the Jesse tree. The ornaments are **symbols**, or things that remind us, of Jesus and His coming. This crown I'm painting is a sign that Jesus is the coming King."

Meg held up the wooden chalice ornament that she was painting. "This is a symbol of Emmanuel, or 'God with Us,' because Jesus is with us in a special way at Holy Communion. We put these on the Jesse tree when we read the 'O Antiphons.'"

"I get it," Barbie said, "and then you put up the Christmas tree?"

"No, no," Greg shook his head firmly and pointed to the **creche** next to the Jesse tree, "'cuz that would mean you forgot the dog in the manger."

"The dog in the manger?" Now Barbie was really confused. "Are *Aesop's Fables* part of your Christmas, too?"

"What Greg means," Meg smiled, "is that his favorite animal from the Nativity set is the shepherds' sheep dog.

"As Christmas gets closer, we put up the creche. Each day we add more people and animals. They all wait in darkness for Jesus, the Light of the World. We don't turn on the bright star over the creche until Baby Jesus comes, and He comes last, just before we leave for Midnight Mass."

"Midnight Mass?" Barbie wondered in surprise. "You mean you get to stay up until midnight? My parents would never let me stay up that late. You are lucky."

"Oh, we're more than lucky," Seth offered. "We're blessed. And there's more.

"On Christmas morning, we get to eat anything we want for breakfast, and sticky cinnamon rolls with icing, and even Christmas candy. Dad says those are reminders of Jesus, the Bread of Heaven, having all sweetness within Him.

"And, once Christmas Day comes, we have almost two weeks of Christmas."

"Two weeks!" Barbie's mouth dropped open in amazement. "We only get one day!"

"Well, we each open just one present on Christmas," Meg said, "because we want to remember that Jesus is the best and most lasting Christmas Present of all. But for almost two weeks, we all take turns opening a present every day.

"And Mom cooks something special every day of Christmas, like white divinity fudge for Mary's purity on the Solemnity of Mary, Mother of God. And on the Feast of the Holy Family, our family goes out to dinner and then we come home and have a video and popcorn night, and then on Holy Innocents' we take cute baby clothes to the Pregnancy Center. And we get to assist at Holy Mass all those days, too."

Meg stopped to catch her breath.

"And then on Epiphany, we have a big crown cake with chocolate coins covered in gold foil. The coins remind us to treasure the right things, and make us think of the gifts the Three Kings gave to Jesus on Epiphany."

"Epiphany?" Barbie shook her head. "We don't have that at our house, either."

"Yah," Greg nodded, "that's when the dog in the manger chases the Wise Men's camels to the Baby Jesus."

"Well, it was really a star that led the way, but you get the idea," Seth corrected. "And that's when we finish opening our presents, because it's the day that the Three Kings brought presents to Jesus, and the world found the King of Kings."

"Advent, and wreaths, and Jesse trees, and Midnight Mass, and two weeks of Christmas, and Epiphany." Barbie's eyes were wide with wonder.

"You guys sure are lucky."

"Blessed," said Meg and Seth together, "blessed."

"...they saw the child with Mary his mother, and they fell down and worshiped him. Then, opening their treasures, they offered him gifts..." —*Matt. 2:11*

"For where your treasure is, there will your heart be also." —*Lk. 12:34*

New Vocabulary

velvet: very soft fabric
symbols: 'signs' that remind us of something
creche: manger scene

Questions

1. Why did the Peterson's open only one gift at Christmas?
2. When Meg explained about the Three Kings cake, she said, "The coins remind us to _____."
3. Who do you think had a better Advent and Christmas season: Barbie's family, or the Peterson's? Why?

Seth's Pane-ful Accident

Seth planted his feet firmly in the cow pasture's wet, dead grass. He slapped his baseball cap firmly on his head, and blinked the sun from his eyes.

"Throw that baby right here!" Seth pumped his bat up and down, shouting to his friend, Nate. "Let's get an early start on baseball season!"

Nate smacked the grass and dirt-stained baseball into the palm of his leather glove and squinted at Seth.

"Aw, I bet you swing and miss," he teased.

"You just try me. I'm gonna whack that ball clear to the end of the pasture."

Some distance behind the boys, Dad was carrying an armload of firewood into the house.

"Go for it, Seth!" Dad bellowed. "Pop it right to the end of the field!"

"Yah, Seth, you pop that ball!" Greg cheered from his **perch** on top of the pasture gate.

Nate twisted his arm as far behind his head as he could, and then rocketed the ball toward the waiting bat.

As Dad boomed encouragement, Seth turned his body and swung the bat with all his might.

The bat slammed into the ball, driving it into a high, crazy spin that ended only when the baseball crashed through Mom and Dad's bedroom window.

Dad had seen the whole thing. So had Greg, who dropped off the gate and came running.

"Boy, oh, boy, Seth, you don't usually break things as good as I do," Greg comforted his big brother.

Seth was shocked. He stood, frozen, staring at the broken glass. The bat slipped from his fingers to the muddy ground.

"I don't know what happened, Dad. Honest! I was hitting toward the pasture, but the ball went backwards to the house. I'm really, really sorry. I didn't mean to do it!"

Dad had dumped the firewood on the porch steps, and was now eyeing the **shattered** glass.

"It's OK, son. I can **replace** the glass. I'll pick up a new piece on my way home from work tomorrow."

"But I feel awful about it, Dad," squirmed Seth, "like it's a sin or something."

Dad turned away from the damaged **pane** to face Seth. "Well, I'm not exactly happy that the ball went through the window, but it was an accident. You weren't being careless, and you didn't mean to do it. You didn't plan to break the window. In fact, you had permission to play baseball in the pasture. Who would have thought that the ball would fly backwards this far?

"No, it was not something you chose to do. It was not **deliberate**. It was not a sin, but an accident.

"I can put a board over this to keep out the cold and rain. Tomorrow, I'll replace the glass. Don't worry about it.

"C'mon. You and Nate can help me carry the plywood and nails."

Soon, Dad and the boys had a piece of wood in place over the empty spot in the window.

The next day, Dad brought a cardboard-covered pane of glass with him when he came home from work. He would repair the window after dinner, but now it was time to fill some growling stomachs.

The Peterson family sat down to their evening meal. It seemed that they had barely finished the blessing when Greg scraped the last bit of gravy from his plate.

"I'm all done, Daddy. Can I watch you fix the window?"

"Yes, Greg, but I've just started my dinner. We'll repair the window when I've finished my meal."

Greg wiggled in his seat. "Then, please may I be excused? I'm going to go play with Jack."

Greg bounced from his chair, threw his dishes into the sink, and ran outside into the rain without his jacket.

He slid the dripping roof from the guinea pig cage and opened the wire lid.

"Jack, it is too wet out here." Greg pulled his furry friend from the cozy cage. "I will find a dry place where you can run around."

A short time later, Greg was back in the dining room, twisting his fingers in his damp hair as he watched Dad swallow a last bite of garlic bread.

"Daddy?" Greg chewed the end of a fingernail and looked at his toes.

"I think maybe I kinda did one of Seth's accidents. Did you know that when you walk on that big piece of cardboard on the floor of your pickup, it goes 'crunch, crunch'?"

Dear Reader, do you know the difference between an actual sin and something that is truly an accident?

Sometimes children worry that they have sinned, even when they have not. If you are ever unsure whether something is an accident or a sin, remember the depths of God's mercy. Then, go to Confession and talk with your priest. Jesus has called him there to help you.

"For the Lord is compassionate and merciful; he forgives sins and saves in time of affliction." —Sir. 2:11

New Vocabulary

perch: a place to sit
shattered: broken into small pieces
replace: to put something back
pane: piece of window glass
deliberate: on purpose

Questions

1. List at least four of the reasons Dad gave to show Seth that breaking the window was not an actual sin.
2. Look in your catechism and find out the necessary conditions for venial sin, and for mortal sin.

Happy Holy-days

"Greg," Mother called, "be sure to find your math paper before we leave for church, so you can correct it first thing tomorrow."

"OK, Mommy. Beat you to the car!" Greg yelled as he looked at Meg over his shoulder, and shot out the door.

As the back door slammed, Meg heard a **muffled** 'thump,' a crashing metal noise, and Barbie's angry voice outside.

"Don't you *ever* watch where you're going, Greg?"

"Sure, I watch my going. How come you are lying down on my sidewalk with your bike?"

"Because you flattened me, that's why!"

"I'm sorry, Barbie." Greg apologized, helping Barbie to her feet. "I never saw you. I won't flatten you anymore ever again," he promised as he raced to the van.

"Until next time," Barbie groaned.

Meg, pulling Becca behind her, hurried outside to check on her friend. "I'm sorry Barbie, Greg was in a hurry."

"He's always in a hurry," Barbie grumbled as she lifted her bike upright. "Like a hurry-cane, only hurricanes don't wreck as much stuff as Greg.

"How come you guys are all dressed up, anyway? I was coming over to see if you wanted to ride bikes, but where are you going?"

"Don't you know? It's the Solemnity of Mary, Mother of God! We get to go to church today!"

"Again? But today is Tuesday," Barbie said. "Who wants to go to church on Tuesday?"

"We do!" Dad answered as he and Mother stepped off the porch. "It's a great day to celebrate with Our Lord and Lady, and a great start to a new year. After Holy Mass, we'll come home to hot chocolate and divinity fudge."

Dad pulled the car keys from his jacket pocket. "Would you like to join us after Mass, if it's OK with your parents? We should be home by 10:30 this morning."

"Sure!" Barbie nodded in surprise. "Nobody at my house is even up yet."

"See you then!" Mother called as she slid the van's door closed.

"Holidays really started out as holy-days, didn't they, Dad?" Seth asked as he took his seatbelt away from Greg and fastened it. "I like Catholic calendars, because they have more 'holidays' than a regular calendar."

Devotional Stories

"Yeah, I'm glad we get to go to Holy Mass more than just Sundays." Meg took a holy card from her purse. The colored drawing of a girl dressed all in white lace, hands folded, waiting at the altar rail to receive Jesus, her Best Friend, made Meg feel all warm inside. "It seems like I waited forever for First Penance and First Holy Communion. Now I can go anytime."

In the back seat, Greg smacked his lips. "An' I like going to Mass and then getting a big dinner, like last week at Christmas."

"That's probably why holy days are usually called feast days, too, isn't it, Daddy?" asked Meg.

"That's a good point, Meg," Dad said as he backed the van out of the driveway. "Remember when Mom called you for Christmas dinner, for the great feast?"

"I 'member the sweet potatoes," Becca said as she felt under her carseat for forgotten donut crumbs from Sundays past. "The ones with those puffy brown marshmallows on top."

"When Mother announced that it was time to eat those delicious foods," Dad asked, "did anybody grumble, 'Aw, do I *have* to come to dinner, do I *have* to eat?'"

"No, Daddy, I *wanted* to eat all that yummy stuff," Becca replied as she licked her fingers, "'cuz Mommy fixes the best food."

"I get it," Meg said. She waved as their van passed Barbie, pedaling her bike home. "It's like

for Little Folks Too

Holy Mass. God **prepares** the very best for us: Himself. In my mind, it's not a 'have to,' but a 'want to.' Like, how fast can I get there?"

"Yeah, like Mom's good food makes your body grow healthy," Seth thought aloud, "Holy Eucharist makes our souls grow healthy. It's a great Present given to us. Who would want to turn Him down?"

"If someone asked me, would I like to have more birthdays than just one every year," Meg added, "I'd say, 'You bet!' You can never have too many special days."

"Yes, there is so much to celebrate in our Faith," Mother agreed. "I've often thought that making the Annunciation a Holy Day of Obligation would be a good way to honor the unborn Jesus and Our Lady.

"And Greg," Mother said as she glanced in the car mirror and saw Greg leaning forward in his seat, tying Becca's braids in a knot, "you need to find something else to play with."

Greg obediently opened the ash tray, looking for his ping-pong balls. But, instead of ping-pong balls, he found a wadded-up piece of paper. So that's where his math paper with the red marks had been hiding!

Today was 'no school,' because of the holy day, but that paper would be waiting for him first thing tomorrow. Ideas popped like popcorn inside Greg's head.

"Mommy, you always say 'no school' on holy days, 'cuz Mass is more important," Greg chirped.

"Can you make every day a holy day?"

"I was glad when they said to me, 'Let us go to the house of the LORD!'" —Ps. 122:1

"How lovely is thy dwelling place, O LORD of hosts! My soul longs, yes, faints for the courts of the LORD; my heart and flesh sing for joy to the living God. Even the sparrow finds a home, and the swallow a nest for herself, where she may lay her young, at thy altars, O LORD of hosts, my King and my God. Blessed are those who dwell in thy house, ever singing thy praise!"
—Ps. 84:1-4

New Vocabulary

muffled: made a sound more quiet
prepares: fixes, or makes something ready

Questions

1. The Peterson's were going to Holy Mass to celebrate what special day?
2. Seth said, "Holidays really started out as _____."
3. Which day did Mother think would be a good Holy Day of Obligation?

For Discussion

What are some ways that you can make every day a holy day?

In God's Good Time

Dad pushed one last chunk of firewood into the crackling flames and closed the heavy woodstove door. He rose to his feet, brushing bits of bark from his hands. "I'm sure looking forward to summer," Dad remarked.

Across the room, the Peterson children were having school time. Becca was under the dining table, coloring a page in *My Coloring Book of Catholic Heroes*. "I wanna go swimming in the creek, like St. Christopher," she announced as she crawled out from under the table. "Mama, where is my bathing suit?"

Mother laughed. "Oh, Becca, it's freezing outside. You have to be **patient** and wait for summer."

"But I want to swim now," Becca pouted.

"All things in God's good time," Mother said.

Becca looked up at Mother and tugged hard at her skirt. "Then maybe can I drive the car?"

"Where did *that* idea come from?" Mother shook her head and smiled at her youngest daughter.

"Oh, she's been saying that she wants to drive ever since the cousins visited us," Meg offered as she pushed her math workbook across the table. "Seth, would you check my math problems for me?"

"Sure, Meg." Seth opened Meg's math book to the answer key page. "Yah, Becca thinks it's pretty neat that Madeleine is learning to drive, and Thomas starts driving lessons next year. She doesn't get it that the cousins are a lot older than she is."

"But Meg told me that they aren't growed up yet. They are kids, too." Becca argued. "I wanna drive, like they do."

"Look, Becca." Meg pointed to Greg, who was making a long line of orange and green counting cubes next to his wrinkled math worksheets. "See how Greg is doing his math paper? He still has to use helpers to figure out his math problems. After he practices that way for a while, then he will know the answers in his head, like I do.

"And when I'm older, if I work hard, then I can do **division**, like Seth. But I have to learn a lot more math first. And you have to learn lots and lots of stuff before you can drive."

"It's sort of like the sacraments, isn't it?" Seth thought aloud. "We have to be baptized before we can go to confession, and then we need confession before we receive Holy Communion, and then we have to be all grown up for Holy Matrimony or Holy Orders. Each step helps us get ready for the next one." Seth pushed Meg's workbook back across the table. "You missed two."

"I guess I need more practice on my steps," Meg said. "Thanks, Seth."

"I don't wanna do steps," **mumbled** Becca. "I wanna drive."

Dad had been listening as he warmed his hands over the woodstove. Now he called Becca to him. "Becca, can you pick up this chunk of wood in the woodbox?"

"No, Daddy, I am not big enough."

"That's just it, Becca. You aren't big enough. You have many years of growing and learning ahead. You are a **precious** child, but you are still a child.

"Right now, you have Daddy and Mommy to do the driving, to protect you, and help you learn good things, godly things.

"You will drive someday. But now you must be patient and work hard at learning things that will help you be ready to drive when the time comes."

"Like the Sacrament of Penance gets us ready for Holy Communion, and addition gets us ready for **multiplication**," Meg reminded.

"Yes," continued Dad, "all in God's good time, and in His proper order. You know, Becca, that Madeleine is fifteen years old." Dad squatted down and wrapped his arm around Becca's small shoulders. "And how old will you be on your next birthday?"

"I think," Becca stuck out her lower lip, "maybe I'll be fifteen."

"When I was a child, I spoke like a child, I thought like a child, I reasoned like a child...."   —*1 Cor.13:11*

New Vocabulary

remarked: said

patient: patience is a virtue that helps us cheerfully to wait for things, even through sufferings, for love of God and neighbor

division: a type of math related to multiplication

mumbled: spoke softly in a pouty voice

precious: very valuable

multiplication: a type of math related to division

Questions

1. Mother said: "All things in _____."
2. Seth said, "Each step helps us _____."
3. Why couldn't Becca pick up the chunk of wood in the woodbox?

For Discussion

St. Monica prayed that her son, Augustine, would follow Jesus and His Church. Augustine had many 'things' that he thought would make him happy, but none of them would make him happy for very long or help him win Heaven.

St. Monica waited many, many years, for Augustine to change, but she patiently trusted God. In time, her prayers were answered. Augustine became a great hero of the Catholic Church, and a saint.

Think of a time when you waited patiently for something that you wanted very much. Was the thing that you wanted very important, or does it seem a little thing, now?

When we patiently trust in God's providence, He provides all the good things that we need to get to Heaven, the happiest 'thing' of all.

Jesus' Chore Chart

"Greg, why are you stacking the dirty cereal bowls in the sink?" asked Meg. "It's my turn to wash breakfast dishes this week. Check the chore chart."

"I think it's my turn," Greg replied as he filled the sink with hot water, "because the person who washes dishes gets to lick out that frosting bowl."

"I'm telling," said Meg.

"OK," Greg said as he hopped **hastily** off the kitchen stool pulled up next to the sink, "I will look at the chore chart one more time. Maybe I didn't read it right."

"Greg, you know you can't read yet. Besides, every chore has a picture by it so you and Becca can tell what it is."

"Well," Greg squinted at the chore chart stuck with magnets on the side of the refrigerator, "I think this picture by my name looks like a dish."

"Greg, that's a dust pan. You know you are supposed to sweep under the table and by the back door.

"And you and Seth have wash to fold, too, see?" Meg pointed to the picture of a washing machine on the chart. "Anyway, let's hurry and finish our chores. That way we have time to play before school."

Later that afternoon, Seth and Greg were in the living room, folding and stacking the clean wash into towers on the sofa. Seth heard a knock at the front door, and answered with a bath towel over his arm.

"Mrs. Blake! Please come in. Nate told me that you were going to come over today to pick up the cake for the church bake sale.

"Have a seat and I'll get Mom.

"Mom!" Seth called, and then returned to folding the wash.

"Hi, Kate!" Mother greeted their neighbor, "I'm running behind this afternoon. The cake is frosted but I still need to chop and sprinkle walnuts on top. Do you have a few minutes?"

"Sure," answered Mrs. Blake. "We can visit while I wait."

She looked back at the boys folding the washcloths. "With that towel in his hands, I thought I'd caught Seth heading to the shower," she laughed. "Your boys are sure good about doing chores without grumbling."

"I used to grumble," Greg offered, "but Seth told me I shouldn't, because we all help each other so it's easy. Seth said that Jesus did all the chores by Himself when He was a Child, but He still did His jobs cheerfully."

Mrs. Blake asked, "Did you read that in the Catechism?"

"No," Greg said seriously, "Jesus read it on His chore chart. He got *all* the chores because He didn't have any brothers or sisters."

Mrs. Blake's eyes twinkled. "Well, I'm sure He's pleased that you do your chores with a happy heart."

Mother carefully tucked plastic wrap around the chocolate-frosted cake and under the cake plate. "It also has something to do with snack time. Mike reminds the kids of the verse that says if you don't work, you don't eat.

"But I have to add that I'm really proud of the kids because they do their chores **independently** most of the time. Mike checks every day to make sure that the chores are done, and without my reminding anybody."

Mother carefully fit the cake into a cardboard box. "And, if they have done all their independent school work without a reminder, and their chores, too, Mike pays them a dollar for the week."

"Aha!" Mrs. Blake said, "Money always helps."

"Oh, it's not what you think," Mother corrected. "The children don't keep the money. They decided to send all their chore money to the SOLTs* to help **fund** a home for homeless children in Mexico. When the children make it through the whole month without a check mark, Mike **matches** the money they earn."

"But all I got so far is the money," Greg sighed as he added another washcloth to the tower.

"I don't know why Daddy won't give me the matches."

*SOLTs: Society of Our Lady of the Most Holy Trinity, with missions in Texas, Belize, Mexico, and other countries

"If any one will not work, let him not eat." —*2 Thess. 3:10*

"Do all things without grumbling..." —*Phil. 2:14*

New Vocabulary

hastily: quickly; in a hurry
independently: doing something by yourself, without being told to
fund: to pay for
matches: in this case, to add more money equal to the money given for doing chores

Questions

1. Why did Greg want to do dishes?
2. Why did Meg want to finish chores quickly?
3. How did the children spend the money they earned for doing their chores?
4. Mother said, "Mike matches the money they earn." Greg said, "I don't know why Daddy won't give me the matches." Does the word 'matches' mean the same thing in these two sentences?

Becca Digs a Pit

"**M**omma!" Meg called in an angry voice as she raced into the kitchen, "Becca ate all my wintergreen candy! I had a whole roll of candy when we got home from town an hour ago. Now there is only one piece left!"

"Oh, dear," Momma lowered the canning jar that she was washing into the soapy suds and dried her hands on her apron. "Let's go take a look."

"Becca?" Mother called as she entered the girls' room, "Where are you?"

"She's right here." Meg grabbed the edge of Becca's quilt and jerked it into the air, pointing at her little sister, hiding underneath her bed.

"Oh, Becca," Mother said. "You bought your own roll of candy when we were at the store! You didn't really take Meg's candy, too, did you?"

Silently, Becca shook her head solemnly from side to side.

"But, if you didn't take it, where is the candy?" asked Mother.

Becca swallowed hard and, in a choked voice, answered, "In my t'roat."

"Becca, you know that we don't take things that belong to other people. You should have asked permission if you wanted to try a piece of Meg's candy. And when I asked you if you had taken the candy, you lied."

"No, Mommy, I didn't lie," Becca argued, "I just shook my head."

"Then you lied with your head. Come out from under the bed. Tell Meg you're sorry and..."

Mother thought a moment, and looked about the room. She spotted Becca's unopened roll of cherry candy, sitting on her dresser.

"...get your roll of candy and give it to Meg. It is hers now.

"And, next time, be sure to ask permission before you use or take anything that doesn't belong to you."

The following morning, breakfast had been eaten, the dishes cleared away, and the children had returned to the table with their schoolwork.

"OK, Greg," Meg said as she held a simple addition flashcard up for Greg. "What is two plus *yuck!?*

"Mom! There is sticky stuff all over the back of this flashcard, and all over the table at Greg's place," Meg cried. "It looks like chocolate pudding from last night!"

"Yummy," said Greg as he wiped his finger over the sweet, sticky spot. "I like two plus yuck."

Mother had been reading **instructions** from Seth's spelling book. Now she looked at the table and saw cinnamon toast crumbs in the middle of the plastic tablecloth, and yellow bits of scrambled egg at Becca's place.

"Whose turn is it to wipe the table this week?" Mother asked. "Whose name is on the chore chart?"

"I don't feel so good," said Becca as she slipped out of her chair and rushed from the room. "I think I need to lie down."

Mother followed Becca down the hall, only to find Becca sitting in the middle of her unmade bed.

"Becca! You didn't wipe the table, and you didn't make your bed before breakfast!"

"But I felt so sick, Mommy, I couldn't do my chores. Feel my head."

Mother felt Becca's cool forehead. "Hmmm. Yes, I think you need to go to bed right now, since you are so sick that you couldn't make your bed or wipe the table last night or this morning. We'll see how you feel at lunchtime."

By lunchtime, Becca had grown very tired of being in the bedroom by herself. She had not realized that staying in bed all morning could be so boring!

At long last, Mother called her for lunch.

"Becca, are you feeling well enough to eat something? I've fixed chicken salad sandwiches, and celery sticks stuffed with crunchy peanut butter, and crisp red apple slices dusted with cinnamon sugar."

"Oh, yes, Mama! I feel much better now! I'm coming!"

But when Becca got to the table, she saw at her place a bowl of chicken noodle soup. Pretending to be sick had seemed to be a good trick to get out of chores, but Becca now had a sinking feeling that she had tricked only herself.

Mother told Becca that surely, if she were not well enough to do her small chores, she must not be well enough to eat a regular meal. So, Becca had soup for lunch.

A few days later, Becca was playing outdoors when she found a fuzzy black and brown caterpillar sleeping under some dead leaves by the porch. What tiny little feet God had made for him! Perhaps there were even tinier toes on those tiny feet!

Maybe Mother would let her use the **magnifying glass** so she could see his little feet better, Becca thought, but first she would be sure to ask permission. She did not want to get in trouble again, and she really did want to please Jesus by being **obedient**.

Soon, Becca was back, sitting on the porch steps, happily **peering** through the magnifying glass at the hairy caterpillar, at the concrete steps, at the dirt, and at the lines crossing the palm of her hand. What wonders there were in God's creation!

Becca thought of the cows' stall, and wondered what she might find there to examine. She left the magnifying glass on the porch and set out for the cows' stall to gather more treasures.

In the half-light of the stall, Becca saw Buttercup standing at the wooden manger, chewing a mouthful of leafy hay. For several minutes, Becca watched through the spaces in the rough board fence as the friendly cow stretched her long tongue out for bite after bite of her prickly dinner. Then Becca began stuffing her jacket pockets with treasures to carry back to the porch.

Moments later, sitting on the steps, Becca emptied her pockets. Squinting through the magnifying glass, she studied grains of rolled corn and oats, bits of hay, mouse droppings, and a black beetle that had seen better days. When Becca was finished, she carefully returned the magnifying glass to its box in the toy cupboard.

The next day, when Mother went out to feed the chickens, she saw black spots dotting the floor of the porch. Becca had done much more than examine insects with the magnifying glass! She had burned big spots and little spots, deep into the wooden deck of the porch. Why, Becca could have set the porch on fire!

"Becca!" Mother yelled as she hurried back into the family room. "Come here this minute!"

Becca couldn't think of what she had done wrong, but she came obediently.

"Becca, did you burn holes in the porch with the magnifying glass?"

"No, Mommy, I didn't!"

"Becca, you were the one using the magnifying glass."

"But Mommy," Becca insisted tearfully, "I didn't do it!"

"Oh, Becca, I wish I could believe you, but how can I trust you, when you have lied so many times this week? I am so upset with you! Go sit on time-out while I think about what to do."

Mother had been so angry that she had not seen Greg come into the family room behind her.

"Um, Mommy, you know that glass thingy?" Greg looked at the floor and twisted his fingers around and around in his shirt's buttonholes. "When Becca was in the cows' stall, I got that glass thingy and made smoky holes in some leaves with it like Seth showed me last summer and I guess the holes went through the leaves and made spots in the porch, too." Greg swallowed hard and then bravely finished, "I think it is me that you are mad at, and not Becca."

Dear Reader, think of how much courage it took for Greg to admit what he had done! How pleased Jesus must have been that Greg did what was right, even though he was scared.

Of course, Becca was thankful that Greg had confessed, for Mother immediately apologized to Becca and let her off the stool. And, because of his brave honesty, Greg's only punishment was that he could not use the 'glass thingy' for the next million years.

"He who digs a pit will fall into it, and a stone will come back upon him who starts it rolling." —*Prov. 26:27*

"Do not lie to one another..." —*Col. 3:9*

New Vocabulary

instructions: directions
magnifying glass: a glass lens that makes things look bigger
obedient: doing what you are told to do
peering: looking

Questions

1. What four things did Becca lie about?
2. How did Becca 'dig a pit' that made it so she had soup for lunch instead of what everyone else was eating?
3. Why did Mother think that Becca was lying about not making the burned marks in the porch?
4. Who did make the burned marks on the porch?
5. Did Greg ask permission to use the magnifying glass?
6. Why was it brave of Greg to tell on himself?

For Discussion

Why is it a good idea to ask permission before using or taking something that doesn't belong to you?

Why is it so hard to believe someone who has lied in the past?

 # Living the Gospel, Part I

As the weather man had promised, Friday dawned sunny and warm, breaking winter's clammy chill, if only for a few days.

Not wanting to waste a moment of the Spring-like weekend, by Friday evening the Peterson family was pulling their crowded van into a forested campground, not far from the beach.

The van crept slowly along the park's winding road. Dad peered between the tall, sheltering fir trees, searching for an empty camp site.

"It looks like we're not the only ones who are making good use of the nice weather," Dad commented.

"Wait! There's a good spot, Mike." Mother pointed to an empty campsite between two travel trailers. "See? It has a level place for the tent, an open fire pit, and a picnic table for our meals."

"And it looks like we'll have nice neighbors." Seth waved at a young couple seated at the picnic table next to their travel trailer, on the north side of the empty camping spot. On the south side, an elderly man and woman, followed by a small puppy, were going up the metal steps into their camp trailer.

Dad had barely finished backing the van into their campsite when Greg slid the side door open and jumped out.

"Hi!"

Before Mom could stop him, Greg had bounced through a thin hedge of huckleberry bushes to meet the new 'neighbors.'

"My name is Greg!" He offered his hand to the young man sitting, surprised, at the picnic table. "I'm glad to meet me! What's your name? We are camping here. Are you camping here?"

"Um, yes. I'm Brad, and this is my wife, Tifany. We'll be here until Sunday. And I think your mother wants you."

"Oh, yeah, she wanted me for a long time before I came home to my house. Mama says God wanted me, too, so that's why He made me. And my Daddy says kids are God's reward. Do you gots any kids?"

"That would be totally 'no,'" said Brad, "and here comes your mother."

Mother, with Becca close behind her, pushed the huckleberry branches aside and reached for Greg's hand.

"I hope he hasn't been bothering you," Mother apologized. "He's our friendly one."

Tifany, who could see Seth and Meg unloading sleeping bags on the other side of the bushes, wrinkled her nose at Becca and Mother.

"Just how many kids do you have, anyway? Is that the youngest?" she asked, pointing at Becca.

Mother paused, studying Tifany's face.

"Well," she answered in an extra cheerful voice, "we like to think of her as our middle child.

"It was nice meeting you," Mother smiled over her shoulder as she pushed Greg and Becca ahead of her, back to their camping space.

While Mother heated a pot of hot dogs and baked beans over a smoking fire, Dad and the children worked together to unload the van. Then, the tent was set up on a smooth, sandy spot right next to the parking space.

When the Peterson's gathered around the table to enjoy their dinner as a family, Mother noticed the young couple watching them from their trailer's open window.

"Mike," Mother said in a low voice, "I feel like we're in a zoo, but this time we're the animals."

In an even lower voice, Dad whispered, "Well, let's give 'em their money's worth.

"Greg!" Dad boomed as the sunset beamed orange and pink fingers of light through the towering trees, "it's a beautiful evening in God's beautiful creation. Your turn to say the blessing!"

Over the window, a curtain was pulled shut, except for a little crack.

"...through Christ Our Lord, Amen. In the Name of the Father and of the Son, and of the Holy Spirit, Amen," Greg finished. "Please pass the hot dogs and beans and salad and can I have some grapes?"

"May I have some grapes," Mother corrected, "and no, they are in the cooler, for tomorrow's lunch."

"But I like grapes, Mama," Greg said.

"That's good, because you'll like them even better tomorrow."

"Mike, we have a visitor." Mother nodded pleasantly at the elderly gentleman from the other camp trailer.

"I'm sorry to bother you," said the man, looking around the campsite with a worried expression on his face. "We have a new puppy, who was lonely until we bought a little teddy bear for him to sleep with. The pup came from a large **litter**, and is used to the love and warmth of lots of brothers and sisters."

"Me, too!" chirped Greg.

Dad saw a crack of light from the young couple's trailer as the curtain moved again.

"Anyway, when we drove up today for the weekend, we think maybe the bear fell out of the trailer. It might be lost here in the campground, or it could be anywhere on the road.

"It wouldn't matter so much, but the little fellow always sleeps right beside that teddy bear." In the twilight, the man's eyes searched over the thick carpet of fir needles covering the floor of the campsite, hoping to see the stuffed toy.

"Without that bear, the pup whines, whimpers, and barks. The poor little guy just can't fall asleep without his furry buddy. If we can't find it, I don't think anybody will get any sleep."

"Daddy, Daddy," Greg pulled Dad's sleeve, "he can have my Teddy!"

In a flash, Greg was gone from the picnic bench and unzipping the door of the tent. "He's in my sleeping bag, but I will get him!"

As quickly as he had left, Greg was back.

"Here's Teddy," Greg beamed as he waved the scruffy, one-eyed bear over his head. "Your puppy dog can sleep with him."

"Greg, that's awfully nice of you, but are you sure that you want to give Teddy away?" Dad asked.

"Sure, Daddy." Greg handed his bedtime toy to the surprised gentleman. "I have my brother and sisters to keep me company and love me, but your puppy is all by hisself."

"Well, thank you." The man turned the stuffed animal over in his hands, examining it. "This bear looks a bit like the one we lost. It just might do the trick.

"I didn't think that people cared about anyone but themselves anymore. But I noticed that you folks are religious," the man said as he began to walk back to his trailer. "I guess that makes all the difference."

(to be continued...)

"...sons are a heritage from the LORD, the fruit of the womb a reward. Like arrows in the hand of a warrior are the sons of one's youth. Happy is the man who has his quiver full of them!"
—*Ps. 127:3-5*

"Do not neglect to do good and to share what you have, for such sacrifices are pleasing to God." —*Heb. 13:16*

New Vocabulary

litter: group of babies born to a dog or cat

Questions

1. Why was the puppy lonely when the elderly couple first brought it home?
2. Who did Greg say could 'keep me company'?
3. Why do you think Greg was willing to share his teddy bear?
4. The elderly man said, "I didn't think that people cared about anyone but" who?

For Discussion

In what ways do you think that God's wise plan for children and families helps people learn to think of others?

What are some good things the young couple might have learned about the blessing of families by watching the Peterson's?

Living the Gospel, Part II

Dad stroked Greg's hair fondly as he watched the elderly gentleman, flashlight shining through the darkness onto the sandy path ahead, return to his camping spot.

He opened the door to his travel trailer and, for a short moment, light streamed out across the Peterson's campsite.

In that moment, the children caught a **glimpse** of the puppy, wiggling a happy welcome to the stuffed bear held before him. The door shut, and the campsite was again blanketed with the growing darkness.

"Greggy," Dad said proudly, "you have been living the graces poured out at your baptism today."

"But, Daddy," Greg **objected**, "I didn't pour any water on me, not even very much when I washed my hands."

"No," Dad laughed, "what I meant was that the Church teaches, when we are baptized, that we must live our Faith so others can see it. We are to be missionaries to the love of Jesus Christ, wherever we are.*

"I think you have been a good missionary today."

"Yeah," offered Seth, "kind of like that saying, 'preach the Gospel at all times and, when necessary, use words.'"

"Exactly," Dad nodded. "Well, gang, it's nearly nine o'clock, and I believe your mother's getting Becca ready for bed. It's time for us to join the girls."

By lantern-light, Mother and Meg had spread a row of six cozy, warm sleeping bags on the tent's floor. In their snug shelter, the family prayed a bedtime rosary together, and then it was time to crawl into their **cocoons**.

"OK, everybody," Dad said as he zipped up his sleeping bag, "we're all going to be quiet now, and listen to the night sounds as the forest goes to bed.

"And that's not a suggestion, it's an order."

Through the tent's thin walls came the soft, distant murmur of waves falling against a sandy beach.

Night breezes whispered through the tip tops of the mighty fir trees, brushing against the starry sky far above.

Sleepy peeper frogs, warmed by the false Spring, hummed a lullaby in a nearby cat-tail marsh.

The surrounding woods slept.

"Amaaay-zing grapes," sang Greg, from deep inside his sleeping bag, "how sweet they sound..."

"Greg," Dad growled, "go to sleep."

"Yes, Daddy."

The tent was quiet again, at least until Greg rolled his sleeping bag over Seth.

"GREG, get *OFF*. Dad, make Greg move."

"Greg," Dad growled, "go to sleep."

"DAD!" Meg struggled to sit up in her cocoon. "Greg is sticking his feet in my face!"

"Mike," Mother groaned, "at home, when he rolls over too far, he just falls out of bed. Here, he annoys whomever is sleeping next to him, which seems to be pretty much everybody. At this rate, nobody is going to get any sleep tonight."

Suddenly, doors slammed, and a car motor started at the next campsite. Gravel crunched under tires as the young couple's trailer pulled out and away.

"Hey!" Greg said, "I thought they were going to stay for the whole weekend."

"*Were*, Greg, *were*," Dad sighed. He sat up in his sleeping bag and rubbed his forehead with both hands. "I wish we could get away from the noise and activity as easily. What is it going to take to get you to sleep?"

"Pretty please, Daddy, could I sleep in the van? Pretty please?" begged Greg. "I would have lots of room and Meg's face wouldn't bother my feet."

"Do you think it's safe, Mike?" Mother asked. "But then," she answered her own question, "he would be inches from the tent, and everyone in the campground could hear the van door open and shut if Greg thought about getting up."

"I won't get up, Mama," promised Greg. "I will stay in my sleeping bag and go to sleep."

Dad carried Greg like a sack of groceries, right inside his sleeping bag, to the van. He helped his son get comfortable in the wide back seat and then instructed, "Greg, it is ten o'clock. I know it's not like being at home in your own bed, but it's way past bedtime.

"Not a peep out of you. Shut your eyes. Go to sleep."

Greg nodded silently and, with both hands, pulled the top edge of his sleeping bag over his head as Dad closed the van door.

Quiet returned to the tent, and to the campground. The Peterson family, at long last, slept.

A half moon rose, silvery, above the trees. As the night passed, the moon slid higher in the sky, glowing gently down onto the Peterson's campsite.

Mother dreamed that it was Christmas. The Peterson's were at a church Nativity play, and Greg was dressed like an angel, singing and flapping his wings and jumping up and down on the stage floor. Thump, thump, the floor boards thumped in time to the music.

"Away in a manger, no crib for a bed, the little Lord Jesus lay down His sweet head..."

Mother stirred in her sleep. Now the Wise Men appeared on stage, riding in their travel trailer. The dream was so real...Mother sat up suddenly in her sleeping bag, looking about her in the dark, trying to remember where she was.

Greg was singing Christmas carols, but this was no dream. The thumping was coming from their bouncing van, and the elderly couple's trailer was leaving, with or without the Wise Men.

Awakened by the noises, Dad tripped out of his sleeping bag and through the tent flap into the moonlight. He flung open the van door and roared, "GREG!!!"

"Daddy," a tiny voice answered, "before you say anything, did you hear how quiet that doggy was?"

Dear Reader, in spite of his faults, by his friendly attitude and generous sharing, Greg showed that his Faith wasn't just a Sunday or part-time Faith, but was part of who he was every day, all the time, at home and in public.

And, in a spirit of **charity**, it might be *possible* that the Peterson's 'neighbors' had suddenly remembered during the night that, when they had left home, they forgot to turn off the kitchen stove. It is equally *possible* that sharks like to eat watermelon, and that robins ride bicycles.

*see *Catechism of the Catholic Church* #1270

"Let your light so shine before men, that they may see your good works and give glory to your Father who is in heaven."
—Matt. 5:16

"Preach the Gospel at all times and, when necessary, use words." —*St. Francis of Assisi*

New Vocabulary

glimpse: a quick look
objected: spoke against
cocoon: protective covering in which caterpillars live while changing to butterflies or moths
charity: love that overlooks faults and tries to think the best of people's actions

Questions

1. Dad said, "...the Church teaches, when we are baptized, that we must live our Faith so _____."
2. What did the Peterson's do just before they went to bed?
3. What were some of the night sounds that they heard?

Judging Where to Walk

"**I**'m afraid that you got a 'D' on your math test," Mother said as she passed Meg's paper to her across the table. "You did a great job on adding, but you're still missing the subtraction problems."

Meg **glared** at the red marks on the paper and wished she could tear the test into little pieces.

"I hate subtraction."

"Well, let's go over some of the problems again," Mother suggested. "You were getting them right last week when you checked your answers.

"Do you remember when I showed you how to check the answers?"

"Yeah, I know," mumbled Meg, "cover the top number, then add the bottom number and the old answer. Then uncover the top number. If the new answer is the same as the top number, the old answer is right."

"Why, Meg, I'm surprised at you," Mother said. "You knew how to check your work, but you didn't do it. That's why you missed so many."

"How come you always **criticize** the way I do my work?" Meg muttered.

"Meg, you need to change your **attitude**, or you're going to be writing sentences," Mother warned. "Don't you see that helpful **criticism** is a good thing? Such criticism shows us how to do things right, saving us work and **frustration**.

"If you had taken the time to check your work, this could have been an 'A' paper."

Mother turned to give Greg a hand with his addition, leaving Meg to check over her test.

Meg took a deep breath and asked Blessed Mother to help her calm down. Well, I would rather have an 'A' instead of a 'D,' Meg thought to herself.

If criticism could help her get the answers right, maybe criticism wasn't so bad, after all.

Meg suddenly remembered something that had happened last summer, when she and Becca had been climbing their back yard cherry tree, picking and eating the sweet, ripe fruit.

Mother had been in the kitchen, rolling a buttery circle of dough for a coconut pie. That gave Becca and Meg an idea. Maybe Mother would let them make cherry pies in their little pie pans!

Meg and Becca had picked the juicy cherries, and Mother gave them some left-over pie dough.

The girls were almost ready to put the cherries into the pie pans, when Mother told them that they should take the **pits** out of the cherries first.

But pitting the cherries would take forever! At the time, it seemed that Mother wanted to make more work for them, just like checking the subtraction problems.

As soon as Mother had left the kitchen, Meg and Becca dumped the cherries, pits and all, into the raw pie crusts. The girls sprinkled sugar and cornstarch over the fruit, and then pinched the top crust into place.

How tempting the little pies looked when they came out of the oven, their bright red cherry juice bubbling up through holes in the golden brown crust!

But tasting the dessert taught the lesson that the girls didn't want to hear from Mother.

When the girls popped the first bites of sugary crust and red fruit into their mouths, their teeth gave them the bad news. Why, it was almost like trying to eat a rock pie!

Meg looked again at the math test on the table in front of her.

"Oh, Mom, I'm sorry," Meg apologized. "I guess I just didn't want to do the extra work. But the extra work would have saved me time in the long run. If I'd checked my work during the test, I would have gotten an 'A.' And I wouldn't have all these problems to correct now."

Mom smiled, "That's my smart girl."

"Yeah, helpful criticism kind of reminds me of something that happened with Barbie last summer," Meg said as she began erasing the wrong answers on her paper.

"Greg made a bridge across a shallow part of the creek with an old, rotten board. Barbie came down while we were playing, and she decided that she was going to go across on the board.

"I told her, 'Barbie, you are not being very smart if you try to walk across the creek on that rickety board,' but she wouldn't listen.

"She said, 'You are just chicken. Besides, what's that verse about not judging lest you be not judged? You shouldn't tell me what to do.'"

Meg giggled and continued, "Barbie said, 'You never want to do anything fun,' just before the board broke and she fell into the creek."

Mother couldn't help but laugh. "Well, I'm glad that Barbie didn't get hurt, but I have to admit that's a funny example of helpful criticism. It's also an interesting example of not judging others.

"Of course, we should judge between what is smart and what is not, between what is good and what is evil.

"Now, the Church teaches us not to judge a person's soul, for only God can see what is going on inside. But we can and should judge whether actions themselves are good or bad. If we don't, we might find ourselves walking on rickety boards and falling into the creek, too!"

"Yeah, in the end, I guess helpful criticism and good judgment are better than wet clothes," Meg agreed. She covered the top number on the first subtraction problem that she'd missed. "And I'm going to get an 'A' on my next test."

"Look carefully then how you walk, not as unwise men but as wise..." —Eph. 5:15

"Poverty and disgrace come to him who ignores instruction, but he who heeds reproof is honored." —Prov. 13:18

"...it is my prayer that your love may abound more and more, with knowledge and all discernment, so that you may approve what is excellent, and be pure and blameless for the day of Christ..." —Phil. 1:9-10

New Vocabulary

glared: stared angrily
criticize: to consider and judge between good and bad points
attitude: state of mind
criticism: considering and judging between good and bad points
frustration: discouragement
pits: the hard 'stone' found in the center of cherries, plums, and other fruits

Questions

1. What happened because Meg didn't take the time to check the answers on her test?
2. How did Mother try to help Meg get the right answers in subtraction?
3. When Meg was mad, what did she do to help herself calm down and get control of her attitude?
4. When Mother told the girls to take the pits out of the cherries, was she just being mean, or was she giving them helpful criticism?
5. What happened when the girls didn't listen to Mother's instruction about pitting the cherries?

Will You Trust Me?

"**G**ood Morning!" Mother greeted Seth as she turned the breakfast pancakes on the griddle. "Since Meg is setting the table and Becca is still in the bathroom, would you please take out the trash before breakfast?"

"Sure," Seth replied, opening the cupboard to get out a new trash bag.

"Isn't the house quiet this morning?" Mother hummed a tune to herself, enjoying the peaceful beginning of a new day.

"Where's Greg?"

"Oh, he's still asleep," replied Seth as he tied a knot at the top of the **bulging** garbage sack and headed for the back door.

Mother hummed a moment longer, until warning sirens began to sound inside her head. Greg was *never* 'still asleep.'

"Greg! It's time for breakfast!" Mother called, as Dad came into the kitchen.

There was no answer.

Devotional Stories

"Mike, would you watch the pancakes while I check on Greg?" Mother had already started down the hall. "He must be up to something."

Mother entered the boys' room to see Greg, still sleeping, with his face to the wall. She put her hand on his shoulder and shook him gently.

"Greg. It's time to get up. Greg! *Greg*!!"

Greg was breathing heavily, but he did not awaken. Mother pulled his shoulder so that he would turn over.

Greg's body turned toward Mother, but he was not awake. His eyes were partly open, but he was not seeing anything.

"MIKE!" Mother screamed. "Something is wrong with Greg! He won't wake up!"

Dad thundered down the hall in great leaps. In an instant, he had Greg in his arms and was shouting commands.

"Seth! Meg! Get Becca and get in the van! Jesus, Mary, Joseph, help us!"

In that instant, the family was sucked into a dark, whirling tornado of fear. Only God knew where and when the tornado would stop.

On the way to the hospital, Dad broke every speed limit. As the van swayed from side to side at each curve in the road, Mother held Greg tightly next to her heart.

In the back seats, Becca, still in her pajamas, cried, while Seth and Meg joined Mother and Dad in begging Our Lord for His loving mercy.

Seth and Meg especially asked the **intercession** of Greg's favorite saints, St. Andrew Kim Taegon and the Korean Martyrs.

And then the van squealed to a stop at the emergency room door, and the nurses rushed Greg away.

Through it all, Greg 'slept' his strange and frightening sleep.

The doctors came and went, their white jackets flapping behind them as they burst through the door, asking Dad and Mom question after question.

Had Greg fallen down? Had he hit his head? What was Greg doing before he 'fell asleep'? What had Greg eaten? Could he have eaten something **poisonous**?

Mother's head was a blur of memories. She tried to think. There were the times that Greg had eaten the Christmas ornaments, and the flower bulbs, a tube of toothpaste, and worse. No, she told the doctors, this time she could not think of anything that Greg had eaten. The doctors left, leaving the Peterson's alone in the waiting room.

An hour passed, then two. The doctors were running tests, but Greg was no better.

"Joan, it isn't good for the kids to be here," Dad worried. "How about I get the van and take the rest of the kids home while you stay here with Greg?"

Mother nodded and Dad was out the door.

"Mama," Meg sobbed, "is Greg going to die?"

Mother made a little sound in her throat and pulled Meg close, just as Fr. Antoninus appeared in the waiting room doorway.

"I was in the back with another patient when Greg came in. I've given him the Sacrament of the Anointing of the Sick, and I'm here to tell you to trust in God's mercy. Now, how are you all doing?"

Mother swallowed hard and shook her head. "Trying to trust, Father, trying to trust."

Fr. Antoninus nodded. "I understand. It's scary, isn't it? But we know that God is taking care of Greg as He knows best."

"But why isn't God answering our prayers for Greg?" Meg cried. "We've been praying for a long time, and Greg isn't better. Even the doctors sound worried."

"Meg, remember at the Annunciation," Fr. Antoninus began, "when the Angel Gabriel asked the Virgin Mary if she would be the Mother of the Son of God? She could not see the future, but God asked her to trust the future to Him.

"When we are going through scary or sad times, God asks us, 'Do you trust Me? *Will* you trust Me?'

"God is giving you the chance to say 'Yes' to Him, Meg, just as the Blessed Mother did."

"But I wish I could see what was going to happen first," Meg gulped. "I feel like I am inside a big, black cloud."

"Meg, when the sun is out, and you are playing in your cow pasture, can you tell whether or not the porch light is on, back at the house? No, because the sunlight is so bright and cheery." Fr. Antoninus answered his own question and went on. "In life, sometimes when it's bright and sunny, it's easy to think that we don't need the Light at all.

"But if night falls when you are in the pasture, the porch light is a bright signal in the **distance** to show you the way home. It is the darkness that makes us look for, and see, the Light. So, even though it is scary and dark for you now, look for the Light. He will show you the way."

Seth wiped his eyes and shoved his fists deep into the pockets of his jeans. "What this makes me think of is Good Friday, like from Stations of the Cross last week. 'My God, My God, why have You forsaken Me?' "

"Yes, Seth," Fr. Antoninus agreed. "But, in His **agony**, Jesus still trusted, and very soon came the Resurrection. Today may feel like Good Friday, but we can trust God for the future. No matter what happens, Greg is in God's good hands, and the Resurrection, one way or another, is on the way."

While Mother and the older children talked with Fr. Antoninus, Becca wandered over to the windows to watch for Dad. Her nose was pressed to the cold glass when the van pulled to a stop outside. She called out, "Daddy's here!" just as a doctor came into the waiting room.

"Mrs. Peterson? Your son is awake. He had a very serious **seizure**, and has a terrific headache, but he is awake. And he keeps asking if we've seen Andrew Kim. Is that his brother?"

Dear Reader, you will want to know that Greg went home the next day, with a new medicine, and just as much energy as ever. And the doctor learned something about our very real brothers and sisters in the Communion of Saints.

You will also want to know that Greg never again had another seizure.

"Trust in the LORD with all your heart..." —*Prov. 3:5*

"'I am the light of the world...'" —*Jn. 8:12*

"...and the smoke of the incense rose with the prayers of the saints from the hand of the angel before God." —*Rev. 8:4*

New Vocabulary

bulging: stuffed full and sticking out
intercession: when a person within the Communion of Saints, Suffering, Militant, or Triumphant, prays for another person
poisonous: something that will make you very sick or even kill you if you eat it
distance: far away
agony: great suffering
seizure: a loss of consciousness caused by unusual brain activity

for Little Folks Too

Questions

1. Which sacrament did Greg receive through Fr. Antoninus' hands?
2. Fr. Antoninus said, "It is the darkness that makes us look for, and see, the _____."
3. What Light was Fr. Antoninus talking about?

Too Much of a Good Thing

"I think I'm going to die," Seth moaned as he **clutched** his stomach and rolled from side to side on the living room carpet.

"I think you just gots a tummy ache from stuffing your face with too much pizza pies," Greg offered helpfully.

"Sausage, salami, pepperoni, black olives, tomatoes," Meg counted on her fingers, "green peppers..."

"Oooooo," groaned Seth, "puh-LEEZ, stop!"

"...mushrooms, pineapple, and two kinds of cheese!" Meg finished counting. "That's ten different toppings, and you got them all down."

"Now I just have to *keep* them down," Seth burped. "Excuse me. I guess I overdid it, but it's hard to stop when you are surrounded by so much tempting pizza."

"I think I missed something." Dad walked into the room, carrying two fluffy bed pillows and pillowcases that he'd just taken from the dryer. "How much pizza are we talking about?"

"Nate had boxes and boxes of the stuff for his birthday party, and we were sort of having a contest to see who could eat the most." Seth crossed his eyes and puffed his cheeks out like two matching balloons. "I had at least eleven pieces, but then I lost count."

"That is quite a few slices," Dad agreed. "I'd say this is definitely a case of **disordered** use of pizza."

"A what?" Seth sat up and leaned weakly against the sofa.

"Disordered use. It means that you took something that God made to be good, but used it in a wrong way. God made food for us to be healthy, but we sometimes give in to our desires and use food in an unhealthy way."

"And then maybe you hafta go to the doctor," Greg nodded. He climbed onto the sofa next to Meg and began swinging his legs in Seth's direction.

"Yeah, like you did when you stuck a fat popcorn kernel in your nose," Seth answered, moving over to get away from Greg's kicking feet. "You shoved it so far up there that even Dr. Born had trouble getting it out. Noses are good, and popcorn is good, but that would be a disordered use of popcorn. Right, Dad?"

"More or less. God gave us appetites for food and drink for our good, and for our **pleasure**. But we are sometimes tempted to use our appetites in bad ways. Disordered appetites never satisfy, but lead instead to great unhappiness."

Dad shook the pillows into their pillowcases and continued. "The trick is to use all our appetites in the way that God intended. Only then can we truly enjoy the good things that God has given us."

"And not waste perfectly good popcorn," Seth said over his shoulder to Greg.

"And not have sicky tummy aches like Seth." Greg swung his legs closer to Seth.

"And not **bicker**, because," Dad grinned as he threw the pillows at Greg and Seth, "that's a disordered use of speech."

"Do not follow your base desires, but restrain your appetites."
—*Sir. 5:30*

"God alone satisfies." —*St. Thomas Aquinas*

New Vocabulary

clutched: held onto
disordered: not in the right way
pleasure: enjoyment
bicker: argue

Questions

1. Sometimes we choose things that we think will satisfy us, or make us happy. But those choices only make us happy for a very short time. What did Seth choose to do that he thought would make him happy?
2. Did Seth's choice make him happy in the end?
3. How could Seth have eaten pizza, but in a good way?
4. Dad said, "The trick is to use all our appetites in the way that God intended. Only then can we _____."

He Saw, and He Knows

"One hundred twenty-nine, one hundred thirty, one hundred thirty-one!" Meg counted.

Seth, on his knees, bent over the heavy paper spread out on the floor in front of him.

"OK, let's draw about ten more thorns on this crown," Seth said as his brown marking pen squeaked new thorns onto the poster. "That should be about right for the four of us."

The Peterson children had read about their Lenten activity in *A Year With God*. They were making a big Crown of Thorns poster to stick up on the family room wall. Each time the children made a sacrifice or an act of love, they would color a small flower on the end of a thorn. Then, instead of Good Friday's painful thorns, Jesus would have a beautiful crown of 'sacrifice flowers' by Easter Sunday.

On that day, Dad would have the children 'draw straws' to see who would take the gift of love to Jesus. The person who 'drew' the shortest straw from Dad's hand would fold the poster very small and bring it with him to church. Then, after Holy Mass, he would lay the gift of love at the feet of the Sacred Heart of Jesus.

"What color do you want?" Meg asked as she held the box of colors out to Becca. "Pick one to be your very own color. That way, you know which flowers are yours, so you can keep track of how you are doing."

Becca reached her short fingers into the box and pulled out a light green color.

"This one is mine," she said.

"I'll make yellow flowers," said Seth.

"And I'll take rose pink," said Meg.

"I pick black," said Greg.

"Black?" Meg blinked. "Black is not a very pretty color for flowers."

"Black," Greg answered firmly, "is Jesus' favorite color."

"How do you know?" asked Seth.

"Because Jesus gots black eyeballs," Greg explained, "and He made everybody in the whole world just like Him, with black right in the middle of his eyeballs, too, 'cuz it's His favorite color."

"You win," Seth smiled. "If you want black to please Jesus, that's a good enough reason.

"Now, help me hold this up, and Meg can tape it to the wall. Then we can start taking away Jesus' thorns by making little sacrifices for His sake."

Meg rubbed a piece of tape on one corner of the paper as Seth and Greg held it to the wall. "This poster makes me think about what Father Sean said about Lent. He said it was a good time to practice 'holy math.' We shouldn't just 'take away' stuff for Lent, but we should 'add' good things, too."

Meg reached for another piece of tape, but the tape was gone. She turned around to see Greg behind her, his mouth plastered with tape.

"Greg, what are you doing?"

"Mmmphh, bbmmphh," Greg grunted.

"Oh, I know what he's doing." Seth took the tape from Greg with his free hand and gave it back to Meg.

"Father said that our little sacrifices are done for love of Jesus, so it is best if we don't talk about what we do. We don't do good things to brag about them, but to please Jesus."

Dear Reader, it wasn't long before the bathroom sinks were polished, although a white trail of scouring powder led through the house, from one bathroom to the other.

Soon after, a crooked, green flower bloomed on the poster, at the top of a single thorn.

A few minutes later, the trail of scouring powder had quietly been swept up, and a rose-pink bud opened on the Crown.

The next morning, when Dad climbed into his pickup to go to work, he was surprised to see that the dashboard had been dusted, and the floormats washed.

A yellow daisy blossomed **amid** thorns.

Just before lunchtime, Mother was in the bedroom folding a mountain of wash. When she came into the kitchen to make lunch, she saw a dinner plate teetering on the counter's edge. The dish was piled high with sixteen lumpy, smashed peanut butter sandwiches. Meg was crawling around the kitchen, rag in hand, wiping smears of grape jelly from the floor.

"Why, Meg," Mother asked in surprise, "are we expecting company? That was kind of you to make lunch, but I'm not sure that we can eat so many sandwiches."

"Um, I didn't make lunch, but I'll bet you can guess what nice person did," Meg grinned.

A lopsided black flower, and another pink rosebud, bloomed on the Crown.

Seth sneaked out after dinner one evening to sweep Dad's workshop, and when he came back into the house, he noticed that someone had washed dishes for him.

Pink, green, and yellow petals drifted over the sharp points of the Crown.

When Dad called Greg to help screw the hinges back on the toybox lid, Greg immediately answered, "I'm coming, Daddy," and he really did come right away.

A giant black cabbage grew on top of several thorns.

All through Lent, children discovered that their beds had **mysteriously** been made, mud was swept from the porch, and garbage cans were washed as if by magic. Faithfully, the children kept secret their little acts of love for Jesus. The Crown alone heard soft whispers as flowers were colored.

"My Jesus, I love You," the pink and yellow daisies seemed to echo.

"All for Thee, dear Jesus," **murmured** the green and black blossoms.

And then, it was Easter Sunday. You'll want to know that it was Greg who 'drew' the short straw. He would take the children's 'poster of love' to church, to lay at Jesus' nail-**pierced** feet.

It was Greg who carefully folded the flower-covered Crown, on which not one thorn could be seen.

It was Greg who set the folded poster on his chair at the breakfast table and sat on it, so he wouldn't forget to take it to church.

It was Greg who, as he walked up the church steps, discovered that the poster was still at home on his chair.

It was Greg, who never cried, who **sobbed** to Daddy that he had forgotten and now Jesus would never know about all the acts of love the children had done to make up for the cruel sufferings of His Passion.

And it was Daddy who said, "It's OK, Greggy. Jesus knows. Jesus saw every kind deed and sacrifice. He felt every **consolation**. Even on the Cross, He knew. It's OK. Jesus saw, and Jesus knows."

"...rendering service with a good will as to the Lord and not to men, knowing that whatever good any one does, he will receive the same again from the Lord..." —Eph. 6:7

"Beware of practicing your piety before men in order to be seen by them...your Father who sees in secret will reward you."
—Matt. 6: 1 & 4

New Vocabulary

amid: in the middle of
mysteriously: without explanation
murmured: spoke in a soft voice
pierced: made a hole through
sobbed: cried
consolation: a comfort

Solve the Little Mysteries!

1. Who cleaned the bathroom sinks?
2. Who cleaned up the spilled scouring powder?
3. Who cleaned the pickup?
4. Who made the peanut-butter sandwiches?
5. When it was Seth's turn to wash dishes, who washed dishes for him?

For Discussion

Even though Greg forgot to bring the poster for Jesus, Dad said that Jesus knew every act of love. How did Jesus know?

Sharing 'Most Everything

"**M**ama!" Becca's floppy bunny slippers slapped angrily at the kitchen floor as she marched into the room. "Greg won't share his green truck with me!"

Mother looked up to see Becca's pouting face, and her little fists tightly wrapped around two toy cars. Mother was silent for a moment, as she poured last summer's tomatoes from their canning jar into a pot of bubbling soup.

"Becca, what do you have in your hands?"

"Cars, Mommy," Becca sniffed, wiping her runny nose on her sleeve, "but they aren't *green*!"

"Becca, you and Greg need to learn to share better. If you will wait a while, I'm sure Greg will give you a turn with his green truck. And don't forget to share your cars with him. Now, please get a tissue for your nose and go play."

The bunny slippers stomped loudly back into the family room. Mother turned the soup pot to 'low,' and set her ears to 'high.'

"You are a doo-doo head, and I don't like you anymore ever again." Becca's pouty voice floated into the kitchen.

"Well, you are a noodle-nose an' a boo-boo brain," Greg grunted as he crashed his green truck through the front door of Becca's dollhouse.

"And you are both going to sit in these corners," Mother answered from the doorway, pointing to opposite sides of the room. "You both need to share, to think of each other more than you think of yourselves.

"You also know that we don't call each other names. Becca, you think of three nice things to say about Greg. Greg, you think of three nice things to say about Becca. Then you may both get up and come tell me. After that, you may go back to playing nicely like you usually do.

"Drop your toys right there, and into the corners with you."

For several minutes, the house was silent except for the sound of cold raindrops drumming on the roof.

As delicious, warm soup smells began to drift from the kitchen into the family room, soft giggles from the family room drifted back into the kitchen.

"Doo-doo head and boo-boo brain are ready, Mommy," Greg and Becca giggled as they appeared in the doorway.

Greg started, "She is a good sister and she gots pretty hair and she is nice 'cuz she shared her gum, and I will share 'most everything with her."

"What gum? When was that?" Mother's eyebrows flew up. "Never mind, I don't think I want to know. OK, Greg."

"Becca, it's your turn."

"Greg is nice 'cuz he didn't take my doll's head off today, and he let me play wif Seth's pocket knife and, um," Becca shifted from one foot to the other, searching for **compliment** number three, "...I like his ugly black and blue toenail, and I will share with him," Becca finished.

And share they did.

By Sunday, Becca's sniffles had turned into a **severe** cold. Dad took the rest of the family to Holy Mass, while Mother stayed home with Becca.

When the family returned home, Greg was the first person through the door. Squeezed in his hand was a sticky paper napkin, twisted tightly around a chocolate-frosted donut.

Becca saw the sweet treat and began to cry. "Mama, everybody got donuts after Mass, except for meeeeeeeeeeee," she wailed.

"It's OK, Becca," Greg comforted, dropping the unfortunate donut to the floor as he pulled off his jacket. "I will share with you."

Becca followed Greg into the kitchen, smiling through her tears. "You are a nice brother, Greggy.

"You break the donut in half, and I pick which piece, like Daddy always says, OK?"

Greg carefully marked the donut with a table knife, to make sure the two halves were very nearly **equal** before he cut it. And Becca just as carefully chose her half.

Then the two Peterson children sat under the dining room table and enjoyed their donut pieces together. Although Mother didn't find out until a few days later, true to their promise to 'share 'most everything,' Greg and Becca even took turns licking the frosting from the napkin.

"Let no evil talk come out of your mouths, but only such as is good for edifying...that it may impart grace to those who hear... Let all bitterness and wrath and anger and clamor and slander be put away from you...and be kind to one another, tenderhearted, forgiving one another, as God in Christ forgave you."
—*Eph. 4:29, 31-32*

New Vocabulary

compliment: say something nice about someone or something
severe: very bad
equal: two or more things the same size or weight

Questions

1. Why didn't Becca go to Holy Mass?
2. Mother said, "You both need to share, to think... _____ _____."
3. Even though we didn't hear Dad say it, what sentence tells Dad's rule for helping the children to share treats fairly? Write that sentence.

To Think About

How do you think Mother found out that Greg and Becca had shared the frosting on the napkin?

Steps Leading Nowhere

"**D**addy, can I have some boards and nails?" Greg burst through the workshop door. "I'm going to build a giant treehouse out in the field for me and Buttercup. She likes to watch the cows in Nate's pasture, but they are too far away. She gots to squint to see her friends. But you can see a long way if you are up in the tree."

"You and Buttercup?" Dad laughed as he sharpened the teeth of his chainsaw on the workshop bench. "I don't think a cow could climb that maple tree."

"I know." Greg dragged the toe of his boot through the sawdust on the workshop floor. "That's why I hafta build lots of steps."

With the side of his boot, Greg made little mountains of sawdust. Then he stomped the mountains flat. "I am a hugemongus dinosaur. Can I have some boards and nails?"

"Sure, as long as you promise not to **scatter** them in the driveway," Dad warned. "Just for the field, understand? In fact, the more I think about it, it would be best if I give you a hand."

"Please, Daddy, can I do it by myself?" Greg begged. "You know how to make things all by yourself. I want to make it by myself, just like you."

Dad scratched his chin, thinking of all the things that might go wrong if Greg had no guidelines to keep him on track.

"Ah, well, it might be a good learning experience for you. Let's do it this way," said Dad as he filled a small brown paper sack with nails. "I will draw a simple picture, with directions to follow. If you don't understand, Seth can help explain my directions to you.

"Here are the nails. You can use the boards behind the cows' stall, the ones from the old chicken coop. There are short boards and medium boards and long boards, so you won't need to cut any."

Dad set his rough hand on top of Greg's head to make sure he had Greg's attention. "That means, don't even think of going near a saw. Do you understand?"

"Yes, Daddy," Greg nodded solemnly.

"If you start hauling the boards into the field now, by the time you've finished moving them under the maple tree, I should have your drawing and guidelines on paper."

for Little Folks Too

"Thank you, Daddy!" Greg, his hammer in one hand and a sack of nails in the other, bounced happily through the sawdust piles and out the workshop door.

By the next morning, Greg had more boards than he could possibly use, scattered in a trail across the cows' pasture and piled under the leafy maple. Now it was time to look at the pictures that Daddy had drawn just for him.

Greg turned the paper right side up and then upside down. It was too hard to read the directions, Greg thought. Besides, this picture doesn't have enough steps. I will do it my way and make lots of steps so Buttercup can climb high.

Greg dropped the **sketch** in the wet grass and set to work on his grand dream.

The Peterson's friendly cow watched with interest as the little boy, who fed her apples and sometimes rode on her back, began to nail boards all over the many trunks of the old tree. One of the trunks held a single, high board; another had fifteen boards crowded close together. Still another trunk had boards going around in a circle, all low to the ground.

Buttercup's head turned toward the house at the faint sound of a closing back door. Maybe someone was bringing her an apple.

"Hey, Greg!" Seth called as he climbed the gate and followed a scattered line of boards toward Greg's building project. "How's it going?"

"Just fine." Greg pointed to the boards going in every direction and, at the same time, nowhere. "See my treehouse?"

"Well, I see boards, but I sure don't see a treehouse." Seth shook his head. "Where are the guidelines Dad made to help you?"

"Oh, they were too hard, so I am making it up myself."

"I can tell," Seth answered. "Why don't you show me how you climb the steps, OK?"

"Sure," said Greg as he tried to stand on the circle of boards hugging the bottom of the tree, going nowhere. "Wait a minute. I'll go up there, instead."

Grunting, he tried to climb up the trunk crowded with boards, but it was like trying to climb a door.

Then Greg reached for the single, high board, but could not pull himself up on it. His hands slipped from the board, and Greg plopped to the dirt with a sigh. "Can you help me, Seth? I don't know what's wrong."

"Well, where are the guidelines Dad made for you? There's a reason he sketched it out, you know. He did it to help you, not to make it harder.

"See, Dad knows what he is doing. The way you are doing it is **confusing**, and a little bit dangerous. You made something that sort of looks like steps, but they aren't safe, and they don't go anywhere. If you follow Dad's directions, the steps will be safe and will lead to a treehouse floor."

Greg brushed the dirt and mud off his knees and hands. "Yeah, I guess you're right. I don't want Buttercup to skin her knees." Greg waved a board at the cow, who had been scratching her head on the maple tree. "Go away, Buttercup, so you don't get hurt."

"I don't think you have to worry about Buttercup," said Seth. "But you do need to follow Dad's directions. You can't just make it up as you go along and expect that it will be all right in the end.

"Remember last Sunday when Fr. Sean said that Jesus gives us guidelines because He loves us and wants us to win Heaven? Since the Church speaks for Jesus, when we follow the Church's directions, we are following Jesus.

"The Church shows us the best way to do things, like Dad's guidelines. Dad knows what he is doing, so we listen to his directions. Same way with the Church.

"Your mixed-up boards are like what Father said about Holy Mass. Nobody, not even a priest, is allowed to change the Church's guidelines for Holy Mass, because it could confuse people, and lead in the wrong direction, just like your steps."

"And then," Greg asked, taking a new interest in Dad's sketch, "people would fall out of trees at Mass?"

"A wise son hears his father's instruction, but a scoffer does not listen to rebuke." —*Prov. 13:1*

See also *Catechism of the Catholic Church* #1125, and *Documents of the Second Vatican Council,* Constitution on the Sacred Liturgy, *Sacrosanctum concilium,* nos. 223, 3

New Vocabulary

scatter: spread out everywhere
sketch: drawing
confusing: hard to understand

Questions

1. Why did Dad sketch guidelines for the treehouse?
2. Seth said, "You can't just make it up as you go along and _____."

> **SWIMMING LESSONS!**
>
> Register now
> for
> Intermediate Class
> Call: 266-3300

Big Rivers to Cross

"**B**ut, Daddy," Meg protested, "I already know how to swim. I had swimming lessons last year, and I can swim all the way across our creek.

"*Please* don't make me take swimming lessons again," Meg **pleaded**.

"Honey, you were in Beginners' Class, and you barely passed," Dad answered. "Our small creek is not deep, and you are not a strong swimmer. Some day, you may have big rivers to cross. Then, you will need to know how to swim safely, and without fear, in deeper water."

"But, Daddy," Meg answered tearfully, "I don't want to. I *can't*."

"You're right, Meg. You can't, if you don't try. But I promise you, if you will try your best, in time, you will become a strong swimmer.

"Lessons start tomorrow." Dad gave Meg a friendly squeeze and stroked her bangs out of her eyes. "I'll take late lunch hours the next two weeks so I can come to the pool and cheer you on.

"And, if you start to drown, I'll jump in and drag you out," Dad teased.

"Oh, Daddy." Meg managed a weak smile. "I know you are teasing. But I'm glad I will not be alone."

All too soon, tomorrow had come. Dad sat on the hard, wooden bleachers of the hot, steamy, indoor pool. His eyes searched to find Meg's dark braids among the bobbing heads that all looked alike.

There she was, her long braids dripping, at the edge of the **misty** pool below, right in the middle of a screeching, bouncing crowd of young students.

As the class waited for the swimming teacher, Meg teetered on tip-toes, neck-deep in the splashing water. To her right, two laughing boys were ducking each other. At her left, two more boys were having a **rowdy** water fight, slapping fountains of spray over the shrieking girls.

Meg turned her head away from the heavy showers raining down on her. She squeezed her eyes shut, moved her arms in little circles through the greenish-blue water, and hopped from one foot to the other, trying to keep her chin above the waves, and stay away from the splashing boys.

I really, really hate swimming lessons, Meg thought miserably. I can barely touch bottom here. The water makes my eyes sting. And if they make me swim across the pool, I'm going to drown.

A shrill whistle sounded overhead. "Welcome, **Intermediate** Class," said a loud voice. Meg opened her eyes to see a lady swimming teacher standing to one side, her wrinkled toes curled over the pool's concrete edge. The lady was pointing her silver whistle right at Meg.

"We will begin with a little test to see how well you remember your lessons from Beginners' Class. You are going to swim across the pool, one by one. As each student reaches the far side, I will blow my whistle. When you hear the whistle, the next student in line will please start.

"Please form a line so that we may begin."

I'm going to die, Meg thought as she struggled through the splashing, noisy swimmers to get to the very end of the line. Jesus, Mary, Joseph, help me!

Suddenly, strangely, Meg found herself thinking back to her First Holy Communion! What a happy moment it had been, when Jesus Himself, Almighty God, our Eucharistic Lord, had come to her for the very first time. Meg remembered the joy of knowing that Jesus was with her in a new way, that never-ending Love had come to **dwell** inside her. And Jesus, in all His power and might, would come again and again, each time she received Him in Holy Communion!

Then Meg remembered this morning at breakfast, when Daddy had read to them from *The King of the Golden City*. She could almost hear Daddy's strong voice reading now:

> 'Trust in me and my help. You will grow stronger each time you try. It is to help you to grow strong that I come to you often. By yourself you are very weak but you and I together are more than a match for the enemy.'*

Meg heard the whistle blow and saw that the line was moving quickly. It was almost her turn. She spotted Daddy waving from the bleachers, and Meg was no longer afraid, at least not very much.

She was not alone, for Daddy was here, and Jesus, too. Meg understood that Daddy must have read the paragraph from *The King of the Golden City* just for her. Daddy would not expect her to do something that she could not do, with God's help.

Lord, Meg prayed silently, I know You are with me in every way, to fight sin, to grow in holiness, and even to swim across this huge pool. Please help me now, dear Jesus.

And then the whistle blew. It was Meg's turn.

Dear Reader, have you already guessed that Meg didn't drown after all? Not only that, she discovered something that she hadn't known before. She really could swim all the way across the pool without touching the bottom! When she made up her mind to do it, with God's help, she did.

Years later, Meg also realized something else. When Daddy had told her that she was not a strong swimmer, that some day she might have big rivers to cross, he wasn't just talking about swimming lessons.

"I sought the LORD, and he answered me, and delivered me from all my fears." —Ps. 34:4

New Vocabulary

pleaded: begged
misty: foggy, steamy
rowdy: rough and noisy
miserably: very sadly
Intermediate: not beginning and not advanced; in the middle
dwell: live inside

Questions

1. When Meg told Daddy that she didn't want to swim, that she couldn't swim, he said, "You can't, if you don't _____."
2. At first, what did Meg think would happen to her if she had to swim across the pool?
3. Was Meg alone at the pool? Who was with her?
4. What did Meg remember, that helped her not be afraid anymore?
5. Daddy read, 'It is to help you to grow strong that I come to you often.' How did Jesus 'come often' to strengthen Meg?

For Discussion

When Daddy had told Meg that she was not a strong swimmer, that some day she might have big rivers to cross, he wasn't just talking about swimming lessons. What do you think Daddy had been talking about?

**The King of the Golden City*, by Mother Mary Loyola, published by *Little Way Press,* distributed by *Catholic Heritage Curricula*

Because They Do

"Mrrrowww? Mrrroww?" Butchie-cat pushed his nose into the crack at the bottom of the back door. "Mrrowwwwww?"

Becca twisted the knob above the cat's head and followed the family pet out the door. The warm, Spring sunshine was spilling across the back porch, where Dad was turning on the grill.

"Look, Daddy," Becca pointed to the purring cat, now at Daddy's feet. "Butchie wants a hamburger, too.

"But how did Butchie-cat know that you are making hamburgers?" Becca asked, surprised. "You didn't even bring the hamburgers out to cook yet! How does he know, Daddy? How does he know?"

"Well, honey, he heard me start the fire."

Dad turned the **flame** high and shut the lid on the smoking grill. "Butchie remembers that each time we turn the grill on, it means we will be cooking something good. And we always give him a little piece of hamburger.

"Behavior that is **rewarded** will be **repeated**."

"What does that mean, Daddy?" Becca asked as she climbed onto the porch swing.

"It means that Butchie knows if he comes outside, he will get a treat."

Dad stooped to scratch the friendly cat behind his ears. Butchie closed his golden eyes and lifted his whiskers into what looked awfully like a smile.

"Of course, it also works in **reverse**."

"You mean Butchie will go backwards, Daddy?" Becca quickly scooped Butchie up and put him in her lap. She did not want him to walk backwards, and fall off the edge of the porch!

"No, Becca," Dad laughed. "Remember when we put in the new sliding door, with a screen?"

"One day Butchie scratched at the new screen. Instead of letting Butchie in the back door, Greg let him in through the sliding door.

"When Butchie scratched the screen, he was let in, just like he wanted. His scratching was rewarded, so he started to scratch the screen again when he wanted to come in. But when we never, never let him in that door any more, Butchie stopped scratching it. His behavior was not rewarded any more, so it stopped."

The back door opened and shut behind Seth, who was carrying a dinner plate piled high with raw hamburgers. Butchie jumped down from Becca's lap to rub against Seth's pant legs.

"Butchie learned quickly to stop scratching at the screen when we stopped letting him in that door," Dad said as he set a row of meat patties on the sizzling grill. "If we had broken the rule and let him in even once in a while, he would get what he wanted some of the time. And then he would have kept trying to come in that door."

"That's kinda like me," said Becca, dragging Butchie back into her lap. "I 'member when you 'dopted me, I always frew my bowl on the floor at dinner when I wanted something different to eat. Only you didn't give me what I wanted. You never even said anything. You just took me down from the table right then. An' I couldn't come back!"

"That's right, Becca." Dad gave Becca a pleased smile. "You've gotten to be such a good girl, I'd almost forgotten."

"I didn't forget, Daddy, 'cuz when I didn't frow my bowl, I got dessert." Becca's chubby hand made circles on the front of her yellow polka-dot sundress. "Yummy apple pie, and one time chonklit ice cream."

"Exactly. Your bad behavior was not rewarded. Instead, you got dessert for being good. And what a big girl you are growing up to be!"

"I'm glad I don't frow my bowl anymore," Becca murmured as she **stroked** Butchie's soft, striped fur.

"And even though I was naughty and hadda get down from the table, you loved me anyway."

"Oh, yes, Becca. Always and forever. Daddies and Mommies train their children, not because they don't love them, but because they *do*."

"Train up a child in the way he should go, and when he is old he will not depart from it." —*Prov. 22:6*

"Those whom I love, I reprove and chasten..." —*Rev. 3:19*

New Vocabulary

flame: part of a fire
rewarded: given a treat or a prize for an action
repeated: done again
reverse: backwards, or the opposite direction
stroked: petted

Questions

1. Why did Butchie want to go outside?
2. What did Butchie do to the screen door?

For Discussion

Read Rev. 3:19. How does this verse show the Fatherhood of God?

If God did not 'reprove' and train His dear children, what might happen?

Home, Sweet Home

Seth set the scratchy sheet of sandpaper on the workshop bench and blew a cloud of sawdust from the top of his birdhouse. "What do you think, Dad?"

"I think any swallow would be happy to nest in it. Nice, job, son." Dad rubbed an admiring hand over Seth's woodwork.

"With the weather starting to warm up, we'd better hang that birdhouse today, so it will be ready and waiting when the birds arrive," Dad said. "I'll carry the ladder, and you can bring the hammer and nails.

"And, since the weather is warming up, how would you like to have a camp-over for your birthday next Saturday?" Dad asked. "I can set the tents up in the back yard, and you can roast hot dogs for dinner. How does that sound?"

"All right!" Seth cheered, doing a victory dance as he waved the birdhouse over his head. "How many guys can I invite?"

"I think if we set up both tents, there would be enough room for six boys. After we get this birdhouse nailed up, why don't you go talk with Mom about who you might invite?"

That evening, after Meg had cleared the dinner dishes and Seth had wiped the table, he and Mother began to plan for the birthday camp-over.

"Let's start with your invitation list," Mom suggested as she sat down at the table with paper and pencil. "Dad said the tents will hold six boys, so who would you like to invite?"

"Well, of course, Greg," Seth answered. "And I will take up one space, so that leaves four more boys.

"Nate should be able to come, and probably John Paul, from the Catholic homeschool group. He and I are both supposed to serve at the altar on Sunday, so we could maybe even drive him to church with us after the camp-over."

"That's a good idea, Seth. Now, who else would you like to invite?"

"Well," Seth began to count on his fingers, "I'd like to invite Josh, but he has a baseball game early on Sunday, so he won't be able to come.

"Then there's Mike, but he has karate lessons Saturday evenings, because it's the only free day he has left after soccer practice during the week.

"Pete would have been able to come last month, but he just started track practice after school, and I think they have an 'away meet' at some other school this weekend," Seth finished, holding up three fingers. "That's three people who can't come."

"What about Jeremiah, from your CCD class?" Mother asked. "He seems like such a nice boy."

"Oh, he is," Seth agreed. "I bet he'd like to come, because he told me once about how much fun he had on a camping trip he took with his family, before he started playing sports and stuff. But he's pretty busy now, with scouting and baseball. He has to go to the same baseball game as Josh."

Seth looked at Mother's short invitation list and shook his head a little sadly.

"Everybody is so busy running around to after-school activities that nobody has time just to have fun. They don't even see their families much, except when they're in the car, driving to soccer or something," Seth **commented**.

"Half the time, they aren't at CCD or they miss their turn at altar serving, because they have to go to some kind of practice. It's like they put training their bodies ahead of training their souls."

"Yes, I remember Mrs. Blake telling me that Nate didn't sign up for soccer this year because he said he was tired of living in the car," Mother smiled.

"Sports can be a good thing. You know that, since you play baseball at church now and then. But sometimes we put our hearts into things that are good, and then those good things may slowly take the place of greater treasures.

"Well, I'm sure you and the boys who *can* come to the camp-over will have a good time next Saturday."

And they did.

Seth's birthday soon arrived, along with his friends. With Dad's help, Seth, John Paul, and Nate set up two tents in the back yard: one for three of the boys, and one for Greg.

Greg helped, too. All by himself, he almost made it to the table with a basket of paper plates, napkins, and plastic silverware.

As the twinkling stars came out, and darkness wrapped itself gently around the Peterson's back yard, Dad and the boys roasted sputtering, **plump** hot dogs and gooey marshmallows over a bright campfire.

"Greg," Dad warned, "I'm going to the house for a minute. Stay at the picnic table, and don't go near the fire until I get back."

"Yes, Daddy," Greg nodded seriously as he scraped the last bits of potato salad from his paper plate.

Nate pulled a smoking hot dog off the blackened stick and licked the dripping, spicy juice, running down his wrist. "I'm glad I didn't sign up for soccer this year," he said. "This sure is a tasty hot dog and a fun birthday party. It's a lot better than spending half your life in the car."

"Hey, look, it's light sabers!"

Bright beams bounced and darted across the yard. It was Dad, bringing flashlights for the boys.

"Here's a bit of light for you. I'll drown the fire for the night in another five minutes, and then I'm headed for the house. If you boys need anything else, just holler."

"Thanks, Dad," Seth said. "When you go in, tell Mom thanks for such a great birthday, too. And thanks again for helping me with the birdhouse."

"Oh, did you make that?" John Paul asked as he blew out the flames on his burning marshmallow. "Guess what I saw while we were putting up the tents?

"There were two swallows zooming in and out of that house you and your dad built. It was like they were saying, 'Here's a safe home to raise a happy family.'"

"Home, sweet home," Seth nodded with a thoughtful look on his face. "I think I know just how they feel."

"Train yourself in godliness; for while bodily training is of some value, godliness is of value in every way, as it holds promise for the present life and also for the life to come." —1 Tim.4:7b-8

"For where your treasure is, there will your heart be also."
—Lk. 12:34

See also *Catechism of the Catholic Church* #2289

New Vocabulary

commented: said
plump: fat

Question

1. Why were there only four boys at Seth's camp-over?

For Discussion

In what ways are sports and after-school activities good? In what ways might they be harmful?

Looking Inside

"Mommy," called Greg, "there is a robin building his new house in the pear tree! He is glad that winter is over, too!"

Mother patted the dirt in place around the newly planted rosebush. She looked up from the flower bed to see Greg and Becca, facing each other across the backyard picnic table and blowing soap bubbles in the direction of the pear tree.

"Yes, isn't it fun to see all the birds and little animals coming out?" agreed Mother. "I'm sure you'll discover more of God's creatures before the day is done."

"Greggy," Becca broke in with a sad shake of her black ponytails, "I still can't blow any bubbles." She puffed and puffed at the dripping wand in her hand.

Becca lifted the wand in front of her eyes, trying to see if any bubble soap covered the center circle.

"Here, I will help you," Greg offered as he leaned across the table and blew a hurricane blast at the wand.

"That didn't work either." Becca rubbed bubble soap from her eyes. "And my bottle is empty." Becca's lower lip began to sag.

"I'm sorry, Becca. Here, you can have my bubbles." Greg pushed his bottle of Bubble-Blo across the rough table to Becca. "Now you can practice some more.

"You practice, and I'm going to look for slugs." Greg reached for Becca's empty bottle and slid off the picnic bench.

Half an hour went by. Mother was kneeling in the dirt, pulling dandelions from the flower bed. Greg passed behind her, shaking the bottle of Bubble-Blo.

"Ker-THUD, ker-THUD." Mother could hear the bubble soap sloshing in the bottle as Greg shook it.

"Ker-THUD, ker-THUD."

Mother stopped weeding and looked up. Since when did bubble soap sound like 'ker-THUD'?

"Greg," Mother called to his back as he disappeared around the corner of the cows' stall, "what do you have in that bottle?"

The 'ker-THUD' grew louder as Greg appeared again, still shaking the bottle.

"A snake, Mommy," Greg beamed, "I found a snake."

Just then Meg stuck her head through the back door and shouted, "Mom, 'phone!"

for Little Folks Too

Mother rolled her eyes at Greg and pointed to the porch steps. "Set that bottle down right there until I have a chance to look at that poor fellow."

Mother went into the house, only to hang up the phone and go running back outside when she heard Meg's terrified screams.

"Meg!" Mother flew through the back door. "What's wrong?"

Meg stood on the porch, **trembling**. In her hand was an empty Bubble-blo bottle, but her eyes were on a lumpy garter snake, slithering into the flower bed.

"I was going to blow bubbles," Meg blurted in a shaky voice, "but I don't think I will, now. Who was that on the telephone?"

"That was a reminder that our family **portrait** appointment is tomorrow," Mother answered.

Mother turned to Greg, who had come running when he heard Meg's screams. "I want to make dinner in peace. Please come in now, and wash your hands. And look at that hair. Oh, dear. How am I going to find time to give you a haircut before tomorrow?"

In the kitchen, Meg began to peel carrots at the sink, while Mother filled a deep pot with water.

"What should I wear when we have our picture taken?" Meg wondered aloud.

"Hmmm. Maybe you and Becca could wear your matching blue jumpers with the pink rosebuds. I would really like this to be a nice, normal picture.

The last one we had taken the week after Becca came home, and she wouldn't stop crying.

"I wonder what's taking Greg so long in the bathroom?" Mother began to slice the carrots Meg had peeled. "Honey, would you go check on him?"

A moment later, it wasn't Meg's screams, but her laughter that **echoed** in the hallway.

"Mommy, Mommy," Meg gasped in fits of laughter, "you better come see this."

Mother pushed open the bathroom door as Meg hooted wildly and pointed at Greg.

Greg stood in front of the mirror, a comb in one hand, and a small pair of nail scissors in the other. Little piles of dark brown hair covered the counter, sink, and floor. Nicks and bare patches of skin spotted Greg's head from front to back.

"Mommy, make her quit laughing at me," Greg frowned. "You are busy all the time and don't have time to rest. I can give myself a haircut so I will look fancy for my picture."

Mother stared in speechless shock. "The family portrait," she murmured weakly.

"Oh, Mommy," Meg's laughter rolled on, "it looks like he had a fight with the lawnmower. Our picture is going to look normal, alright."

Dear Reader, you can see why Meg laughed at the way Greg looked. His haircut looked so strange!

If Greg had been out for a walk, someone who didn't know him might have crossed to the other side of the street when they saw him. And if they had, they would have been guilty of judging by appearances, or the way people look on the outside only.

But we can't always tell by the outside what is on the inside, can we? When Meg looked at the Bubble-Blo bottle, she didn't guess that there was something far different than soap inside! She judged by appearance, but her judgment was wrong.

In the same way, Greg may have looked funny on the outside, but on the inside, he was beautiful in God's eyes. Can you think of some reasons why?

"'... for the LORD sees not as man sees; man looks on the outward appearance, but the LORD looks on the heart.'" —1 Sam. 16:7

New Vocabulary

trembling: shaking in fear
portrait: photograph
echoed: sound, bounced back and forth

Questions

1. In what way did Greg show his 'good insides' when Becca ran out of Bubble-Blo?
2. How did Greg try to save Mother some time?

For Discussion

Do you think Meg should have laughed at Greg?

Joy to My Youth

Seth shut the closet door, tightened the **cincture** around his waist and knotted it. He prayed, "Lord, as I serve today at Your altar, let this rope belt remind me of the ropes that tied you at Your Passion."

He looked down at the hem of his **alb** to make sure that he would not step on the robe as he walked. Seth remembered all too well the day that he'd tripped and fallen flat on his face just before Holy Mass, as he walked up the altar steps to light the candles.

He was frowning at his bristling hair in the closet mirror when the **sacristy** door flew open.

"Hey, Nate, I thought you'd never get here." Seth ran a pocket comb through his hair one last time and stuck it through the slit in the side of the alb, down into his slacks' pocket.

"Yeah, I didn't remember until this morning that I was serving today." Nate quickly slipped an alb over his head and checked out the servers' **schedule** as he dressed for Holy Mass.

"Look at this list! Do you know how many days we've served, just because the boys who were scheduled never showed up?" Nate counted the days. "This is the eighth time I've served this month, but my name is only on the list twice. The other six times, I served because no one else would."

"I know what you mean," Seth said quietly. "I wasn't scheduled today at all, but no one was here yet, and it's getting late."

"Aw, I'm sorry that I was late," Nate apologized as he reached for a cincture, "but sometimes I feel like I'm serving all the time. I mean, it's an honor to assist at the Holy Sacrifice, but don't you ever get just a little bit tired of serving almost every Sunday, and during the weekdays, too?"

Seth rubbed a damp paper towel over the toes of his black church shoes before he answered. "Well, I want to give something to Jesus, you know? He suffered and died for me! This is a way that I can say 'thank you' to Him."

"Yah, you're right, I guess." Nate re-tied his shoe laces so they wouldn't look sloppy. "It's just hard when it seems like nobody else cares."

Seth pulled a holy card out of his pocket, turning it so Nate could see the picture of St. John Berchmans on the front side. From the back side, Seth read, "'I will go in to the altar of God, to God Who gives joy to my youth.'"

"That's kind of a cool card." Nate took the shining Sanctus bells from the sacristy cupboard so he could set them in place in the **sanctuary**. "Where did you get it?"

"Do you remember Fr. Pius, the old, old priest with the funny **accent**? He gave me the card when I served for him, the last time before he died. Fr. Pius told me he used to say those words when he was an altar boy, and that's what started him thinking about becoming a priest.

"You said it's hard to serve when it seems like nobody cares," said Seth. "Well, Fr. Pius cared.

"He never talked much about himself, but my dad told me about him, about his life before he came to America. Do you know what happened to him?"

Pulling a clean, folded cloth from the sacristy closet, Nate rubbed a spot off the golden Sanctus bells. "No, what's the story, anyway?"

"Fr. Pius was from Lithuania, over in Europe. During World War II, Father was a young priest. He loved the Holy Sacrifice of the Mass, but when the Nazi army took over his country, they arrested a lot of faithful priests. They threw Fr. Pius into prison because he wouldn't stop offering Mass.

"In prison, the soldiers beat him up. But he told the men that, if they let him go, he would still take care of his people and say Mass, no matter what."

"Boy, he was sure brave," Nate said. "Did they let him go then?"

"No, they locked Fr. Pius in a dark, dirty prison cell, and hardly gave him anything to eat or drink. Many times, the soldiers dragged him out of the cell and tied ropes around his thumbs. They fastened the ropes to the ceiling and pulled, so Fr. Pius was hung by his thumbs.

"After a couple of years, the Nazis began to lose the war. The Soviet army chased the Nazis out of Lithuania, and let Fr. Pius out of that awful prison.

"But the Soviets hated God and His Church, too. So, just a few weeks after they let him loose, they threw Fr. Pius in prison all over again. Only now it was the Soviets who beat him up."

Nate shook his head. "I don't think I could live through that. How did Fr. Pius make it through?"

Seth looked at the holy card, still in his hand. "You know this part about 'giving joy to my youth'? Fr. Pius said knowing that Jesus was right there with him at Holy Mass was his joy, his courage, and his strength. Through all those years in that miserable prison cell, through the hunger, and thirst, and the beatings, the thought of celebrating Holy Mass once again gave him courage.

"Fr. Pius said he knew that, if he could celebrate the great Sacrifice just one more time, that one time would be enough to change the whole world. Because the Holy Mass is Jesus' powerful Sacrifice, still going on, that changed and is still changing hearts and saving souls."

"Boy, that sure makes you think of Holy Mass in a different way, doesn't it?" Nate looked up at the crucifix hanging on the sacristy wall. "And in a few minutes, we get to be part of it.

"Hey, maybe the scheduled server won't show up tomorrow, and I can take his place!"

"...I will go in to the altar of God: to God who giveth joy to my youth." —*Ps. 42:4, Douay-Rheims*

"To me nothing is so consoling, so piercing, so thrilling, so overcoming, as the Mass...It is not a mere form of words—it is a great action, the greatest action that can be on earth."
—*John Henry Cardinal Newman, Loss And Gain*

New Vocabulary

cincture: cord worn around the waist
alb: a long robe worn by altar boys and priests
sacristy: room in which altar boys and priests prepare for Mass
schedule: organized list of names, times, or places
sanctuary: raised part of the church around the altar
accent: speech that sounds odd to the listener because the speaker comes from a different region or country

Questions

1. How many times did Nate assist at Holy Mass in one month?
2. Why did Nate serve more than he was scheduled?
3. What did Seth pull out of his pocket?
4. Fr. Pius told the soldiers that, if they let him go, he would still take care of his people and say Mass, _____.
5. Fr. Pius said that the Holy Mass is Jesus' Sacrifice, still going on, that changed and is still _____.

Find Out

Who is St. John Berchmans? He is the patron of _____.

A Gift that Won't Break

U h-oh.
Greg felt that all-too-**familiar** sinking feeling in the pit of his stomach as he watched Seth's brand-new model airplane crash into the grass and explode into a sprinkling of plastic junk.

Greg stared at his empty hand, hoping that the small fighter jet with the blue Air Force star was somehow still there, safe in his palm. He shut his eyes, and then slowly opened them again, to peek at the terrible crash site through the open bedroom window.

Nope. I did it again, Greg thought sorrowfully. Just like yesterday.

The whole family had been walking downtown, past Oliver's Bike Shop. It had been such a lovely, sunny day that the bike shop owner had lined up a whole row of shiny, new three-speed bikes, for all to see, right next to the sidewalk outside his store.

As the family walked past the shiny bicycles, a sudden **impulse** had grabbed Greg. Before he could tell his hand 'NO!,' the hand had shot out, all by itself, to touch the first bike in line.

How could he have known that the first bicycle would fall over onto the second bike, the second would bang into the third bicycle, the third bicycle smash onto the fourth? That was when Dad heard the **clatter** and grabbed the next falling bike, before the whole row could crash to the sidewalk. It had been 'The Nightmare of Domino Bicycles!'

As Daddy picked up the tangled bikes, he had told Greg that he must remember to *look with his eyes, not with his hands.*

But how could he ever make such a naughty hand behave itself, Greg wondered? He frowned at the naughty hand, held out before him.

And then Seth walked into their bedroom.

"What's wrong with your hand, Greg?" Seth asked, "And why are you standing on my bed, looking out the window?"

Greg jumped nervously off Seth's bed. "Um, you know that airplane you just made, with all the little pieces? You did a good job gluing all the pieces together, huh, Seth?" Greg swallowed hard and started pulling on his fingers. "I bet you could do it again, huh?"

"Oh, no! You *didn't*," Seth cried, looking at the empty spot on his dresser, where his model plane usually sat. "Where is it?"

With a shaky finger, Greg pointed silently out the open window above Seth's bed.

"Every time you touch my stuff, you always break it!" Seth yelled. "Why did you throw my jet plane out the window?"

"I don't know," Greg said, looking miserably at his feet. "It was in my hand and then, suddenly, it flew outside."

"Suddenly!" Seth struggled to control himself. "Greg, you thought about it long enough to open the window. I bet you don't even know what 'suddenly' means!"

Greg brightened, ever so slightly. Seth must not be so mad at him, to ask him such an easy question. "I do, too, know what 'suddenly' means. There's these kids in my CCD class, Andy and Sara, and they had a very old goat—he was a hunnert an' sixteen years old, I think—and he didn't have teeth anymore and he couldn't eat grass and he got skinny, skinny, skinny. And suddenly," Greg said, his voice filled with surprise, "he died!"

Seth slapped his forehead in frustration. "That wouldn't be suddenly, because you would **expect** a skinny, old goat to die a long time before that. 'Suddenly' is when you *don't* expect something to happen right then.

"And, if anybody should *expect* bad things to happen, it's you, Greg." Seth flopped down on his bed and rolled onto his back. He looked at the picture on the wall above his dresser, a framed

for Little Folks Too   181

painting of the Holy Spirit falling as flames at Pentecost.*

Seth sighed as he sat up and shut the window. "You have to learn to stop and think, Greggy. You can't just do whatever you feel like right then. If you let your wild ideas and temptations run your life, instead of your brain, you are always going to be in bigger and bigger trouble.

"Why don't you ask the Holy Spirit for help?" Seth pointed to the painting. "One of the fruits of the Holy Spirit is self-control, you know," Seth reminded Greg. "You just have to ask for the gift and then use it."

"I got gifts for my birthday," Greg offered as he sat down on the boys' wastebasket, "but they are all broke now."

"Well, self-control is a gift that won't break," answered Seth. "In fact, you could turn it into a real gift for other people, too. When you are tempted to do something that you shouldn't, pray to be strong, and then stop yourself. You can make it into a little sacrifice, and offer it up to save souls, especially the souls of people who don't know Jesus.

"Some people never learn to say 'no' to temptations. They don't know why or how to control themselves, and boy do they end up with broken lives. When you say 'no' to yourself, you can offer it up to help those people, and make yourself happy, too."

"I get it now," Greg said, cheerfully rocking back and forth on the wastebasket. "Broked lives and a broked jet plane.

"I am very sorry I smashed your airplane, Seth, but now it will make you happy. Suddenly, you can offer it up to save souls."

"But the fruit of the Spirit is love, joy, peace, patience, kindness, goodness, faithfulness, gentleness, self-control..." —*Gal. 5:22*

"Let not sin therefore reign in your mortal bodies, to make you obey their passions." —*Rom.6:12*

New Vocabulary

familiar: something or someone you know already
impulse: desire to do or have something right now
clatter: loud noise
expect: to know that something will probably happen

Questions

1. As Daddy picked up the tangled bikes, he had told Greg that he must remember to _____.
2. What fruit of the Holy Spirit is mentioned in this story?
3. When we say 'no' to temptation, we can make it into a little sacrifice, and offer it up to do what?

* see Acts 2

Squeaky Clean

Sparkly sunbeams danced through the living room window, painting a bright square on the carpet as Mother vacuumed. She hummed along with the vacuum, glancing out the wide window now and then to watch Seth, Greg, and Becca, chasing each other around the lilac bush in the front yard.

How good it was to see the cheery, warm sunshine, the purple lilacs all abloom, and the soft, new growth on the pine trees, Mother thought. Why, she could almost smell the pine trees, right here in the living room.

Mother drew a deep breath, drawing the wonderful smell of Spring into her lungs.

Wait! Mother realized that the strong smell of pine was inside, not outside, just as a shadow passed behind her into the hallway.

"Greg!" Mother called as she turned off the vacuum. "Greg, what are you up to?"

"I'm in the bathroom, washing up!" Greg's voice came drifting down the hallway.

Devotional Stories

"OK," Mother answered, "but I want to see you when you are done. I smell pine **pitch**."

Seconds later, Greg appeared in the living room.

"Greg!" **squawked** Mother. "You've been climbing the pine trees again, and you are **filthy**!

"What exactly did you wash?"

"My face and arms," Greg answered, lifting his dirty face and arms for Mother to see.

Mother's eyebrows climbed right up her forehead. "What did you get wet?"

"Nothing."

"That's what I thought." Mother placed her hand firmly in the middle of Greg's back, which seemed to be the only clean spot on his body. "Into the kitchen with you. I think we can get most of the pitch off with vegetable oil, and then you need to jump into the tub."

When Seth and Becca came into the house looking for Greg a few minutes later, this is what they heard:

"Ow! Ow! OWWWWW!"

"I'm sorry, Greg," Mother said as she continued scrubbing the sticky pitch from Greg's red skin, "this is the only way to get you clean.

"There you go," Mother rubbed Greg's elbow one last time with the oily rag. "You are almost ready for your bath."

"I think I am scrubbed enough," Greg squirmed. "Do I have to wash my hair, too?"

"Yes," Mother nodded, "but you will like washing your hair. I just bought some new, fruity-smelling banana shampoo, and set it by the tub. Now, go take your bath, and be sure to get wet this time."

As Greg **plodded** down the hallway, Mother called after him, "When we need a good scrubbing the most, is usually when we want it the least."

"That's funny," Seth grinned. "You sound like Fr. Sean in my last confession, when I really didn't want to go, but knew I needed to."

"What do you mean?" asked Mother.

"Well, like you can't hide your sins from God, because He sees and knows everything, but you kind of wish that you didn't have to confess them. Fr. Sean said that when we need to confess the most, is usually when we want to the least."

"So not wanting to go to confession, then," said Mother, "is a sure sign that you need to go?"

"Yup," Seth continued, "confessing our sins is the only sure way to get those ugly, 'sticky sins' all scrubbed away, so we have clean souls that are safely in God's grace. Then we feel all peaceful inside."

"That's a good way to remember how important confession is," Mother agreed. "Let's keep our souls scrubbed, as well as our bodies."

A short time later, Greg appeared, pulling a clean T-shirt over his head as he skipped into the kitchen.

"See, Mommy?" Greg patted his wet hair, sticking out in every direction. "I'm all squeaky clean."

"And don't you feel better after your bath?" smiled Mother.

"Yes, Mommy, but..." Greg used his shirt sleeve to wipe his tongue, "...that banana shampoo tastes yukky."

"Wash me thoroughly from my iniquity, and cleanse me from my sin!" —Ps. 51:2

New Vocabulary

pitch: sticky sap from a tree
squawked: cried out
filthy: very dirty
plodded: walked slowly

Questions

1. How did Greg get dirty?
2. Why did Mother think that Greg would like washing his hair?
3. Seth said that you can't hide your sins from God because what?

Hide and Seek

"*Shhhhhh! Go away, Greg!*" hissed Meg. She put one finger to her lips and, with her other hand, tried to wave Greg away.

It was Sunday, the Lord's Day. On the Lord's Day, the Peterson's morning was joyously filled with the Holy Sacrifice of the Mass, and maybe a trip to the donut shop, too.

Sunday afternoon was family time. When the weather was cold or rainy, the Peterson's would play Catholic board games, sitting on the floor near the warmth of the cozy wood stove. On sunny days like today, the whole Peterson family often rushed outside after lunch for a game of 'Hide and Seek.'

"*You can't hide with me,*" Meg whispered to Greg in the tiniest of voices. In the garage's dim light, she **scurried** to her hiding place behind Dad's pickup.

"Go find a different place to hide." Meg **squatted** on the rough concrete floor, pulled her knees under her chin, and hugged her legs tightly to her chest. "You always snort and laugh and then we get caught right away. You have to be completely quiet when people are looking for you, and you can't be quiet."

"Yes, I can," Greg said loudly.

"No, you can't."

"Yes, I can."

Meg knew that it was useless to argue with Greg. "OK, you can be quiet. But go be quiet someplace else. Daddy is helping Becca count and they will start looking for us any minute. *Go!*"

Meg was surprised to see Greg spin around and run through the open door of the garage into the bright sunshine. She leaned against the pickup's rubber tire and made herself into an even smaller ball.

Meg listened to the driveway gravel crunching under Greg's flying feet, and wondered where he would hide. When he didn't hide with Seth, he almost always 'hid' behind the cows' gate. Greg was easy to catch when he 'hid' behind the wooden gate, because you could see him through the big spaces between the boards.

Now, Dear Reader, can you guess who Dad and Becca caught first?

Will you be surprised if I tell you that it was Seth? He had been hiding by the prickly hay **bales** in the cows' stall when Dad and Becca spotted his red-striped shirt-tail sticking out from behind a bale.

And can you guess who was caught next? I will tell you that it was not Greg. In fact, everyone had been found, except for Greg! And that is where we will return to our story.

"Greg!" shouted Dad as he circled the house, past the cows' stall, past the purple watercolor-and- mustard-stained picnic table, past the leafy cherry tree, past the thick hedge, and back toward the garage. Looking left and right, up and down, Seth, Meg, and Becca followed close on Dad's heels.

"Greg, where are you?" boomed Dad.

Silence. Greg was nowhere to be found.

Dad ran his fingers through his hair, puzzled. This was not at all like Greg. Greg was always in the middle of things, and it was usually easy to tell where he was. Dad liked to say that Greg was 'noise, covered with dirt.'

"Seth and Meg, let's split up," suggested Dad.

"We will find Greg sooner if we look in different places. Becca, you can help me search."

"I'll go check the clubhouse," **volunteered** Seth.

"I'll go check inside the trash cans," offered Meg.

"Greg wouldn't hide in the trash cans, would he?" groaned Dad.

"He did last time."

"Meg, you check the trash cans," Dad shuddered.

Seth cut across the cows' pasture, bellowing Greg's name as the tall grass swished at the legs of his bluejeans. He tugged on the splintery wooden door of the clubhouse. Greg was not inside.

"Greg!" screamed Meg as she passed under the cherry tree. Pinching her nose tightly, she lifted the lids and peeked into the empty trash cans.

Where was Greg? Soon, it would be time for dinner, and Greg was still nowhere to be found.

Could Greg have gone down the road by himself? Dad began to worry. He called Seth and Meg to join him. They would make one last circle around the house. Then they would begin to search for Greg down their country **lane**.

"GREG!" Dad cupped his hands around his mouth and shouted as he again passed under the leafy branches of the cherry tree. "YOU CAN QUIT HIDING AND COME OUT NOW, WHEREVER YOU ARE!"

"OK, Daddy," called a happy voice from the thick branches high overhead.

"Greg!" **exclaimed** Dad, the worry falling from his voice. "...all of those times that we walked right past this tree! Why didn't you answer when we called you before?"

"'Cuz Meg told me I hafta be completely quiet when people are looking for me, and if I answered I wouldn't be completely quiet."

"Oh, Greggy," Dad reached up for his son, scooting backwards down the tree's bumpy trunk. "For a minute there, all I could think of was the scary time when you were in the hospital."

"Yeah, only it was God that sure seemed 'hidden' that time." Seth brushed away the bits of cherry bark that were sprinkling down on his head. "We kept 'seeking' God and 'seeking' Him, but it seemed like He was hiding from us for a while there."

"But He was there all the time, wasn't He?" Meg said as they all headed in to dinner, with Greg wrapped in Dad's strong arms. "Even though He didn't answer right away, He was still there. Just like Greg in the tree."

"Yeah, and we were looking for Greg in all the wrong places," Seth pointed out. "Some people do that, too. They think God isn't there, but they are just looking for Him in the wrong places."

"I think you two could almost write Father's homily for next week." Dad smiled widely at Meg and Seth as he carried Greg through the back door.

"Look for God in all the right places, like in prayer and Holy Mass and in His Word. And, even when He seems hidden and silent, we can trust that our loving God is always, always with us."

" ...whoever would draw near to God must believe that he exists and that he rewards those who seek him." —*Heb. 11:6*

"With my whole heart I seek thee..." —*Ps. 119:10*

New Vocabulary

scurried: quickly scrambled
squatted: sitting on one's heels
bales: big rectangles of hay
volunteered: offered to do something
lane: road
exclaimed: said in a surprised voice

Questions

1. Why didn't Meg want to share her hiding place with Greg?
2. Why did it take so long to find Greg?
3. What might be some 'wrong places' to seek God?
4. What might be some 'right places' to seek God?

Answer Key

As for Me and My House..., p. 1
1. The Peterson family was at church for Holy Mass and Adoration.
2. 'in the right direction'
3. Greg thought he saw a football hanging from the branch, but it was really a hornets' nest.

'C' is for 'Truck,' p. 6
1. history tests
2. the future
3. none of them

'Muffin' Sandwiches, p. 11
1. It means not staying angry for long, but forgiving quickly.
2. Becca might have missed a ride in the wheelbarrow.
3. We are saying that we do not want to be forgiven, either.

The Wise Man, p. 16
1. If anyone asked for treats, Dad would not stop for any.
2. 'when something good came to us, but not beg.'
3. A wise man thinks before he speaks.

It Seemed So Good, p. 20
1. truth
2. Jesus' Church

'My Special Time,' p. 25
1. Meg and Becca helped with the wash.
2. Seth and Greg helped with the wash.
3. My Special Time
4. We never have to wait for God to spend time with us. He eagerly welcomes our visits with Him.

Family Building Blocks, p. 29
1. It wasn't on EWTN, the channel that the Peterson's watched.

2. 'we centered' and 'God centered.'
3. use that time well, to reach out and not shut out.

Tasting Temptation, p. 36
1. She saw frosting on his face and fingers.
2. the sin got worse and worse
3. Our Guardian Angel can help us when we are tempted to sin.

Whining Mosquitos, p. 41
1. David wanted to ride Seth's bike.
2. The bike had fallen on top of David and he'd been hurt.
3. ...why not be happy doing something that you can do?

God's Wise Order, p. 46
1. Becca had been playing with David, and was copying his naughty behavior.
2. The Sacrament of Matrimony
3. to parents

Created for My Glory, p. 51
1. Greg gave Seth his race car, because he had broken Seth's train tracks.
2. God gave Seth his talents.
3. God gave Greg his talents.

Living Examples, p. 56
1. you set an example for the children who are younger.
2. Meg shared her tea set, pushed Becca on the swing, and then showed her how to 'pump.'
3. Becca shared her colors.

A Log Truck for Jesus, p. 61
1. God With Us
2. Jesus
3. give

Mending More than a Top, p. 67
1. affects not only you, but can hurt others, as well.
2. Answers will vary.
3. They were pulled out when Greg pulled on the rope that was wrapped around Jack.

Much More than a Tree, p. 74
1. The Peterson's opened only one gift at Christmas because they wanted to remember that Jesus is the best and most lasting Christmas Present of all.
2. remind us to treasure the right things, and make us think of the gifts the Three Kings gave to Jesus on Epiphany.
3. Answers will vary.

Seth's Pane-ful Accident, p. 80
1.
—Seth wasn't being careless.
—Seth didn't mean to break the window.
—He didn't plan to break the window.
—Seth had permission to play baseball there.
2. Answers will vary.

Happy Holy-days, p. 85
1. the Solemnity of Mary, Mother of God
2. holy days
3. Solemnity of the Annunciation

In God's Good Time, p. 90
1. God's good time
2. get ready for the next one
3. She was not big enough.

Jesus' Chore Chart, p. 95
1. He wanted to lick out the frosting bowl.
2. Meg wanted to have time to play before school.
3. They sent their money to the SOLTs to help fund a home for children.
4. No.

Becca Digs a Pit, p. 99
1.
—taking the candy
—being sick
—making her bed
—wiping the table

2. Because she said that she was sick, her lunch was a lunch that is good for a sick person, instead of the treats that everyone else had for lunch.
3. Mother thought that Becca was lying, because she had lied before.
4. Greg made the burned marks on the porch.
5. Greg didn't ask permission to use the magnifying glass.
6. Greg was brave to tell on himself, because he knew that he could get in trouble, but he was still willing to do what was right. It was not right for Becca to be in trouble for something that he had done.

Living the Gospel, Part I, p. 106
1. The puppy came from a large litter of pups, and missed its brothers and sisters.
2. his brothers and sisters
3. Answers will vary
4. themselves

Living the Gospel, Part II, p. 112
1. so others can see it
2. The Peterson's prayed a bedtime rosary just before bed.
3. distant waves, night breezes, and peeper frogs

Judging Where to Walk, p. 118
1. Meg got a 'D' on her test.
2. Mother showed Meg how to check her answers.
3. She took a deep breath and asked the Blessed Mother for help.
4. When Mother told the girls to take the pits out, she was giving helpful criticism.
5. The girls couldn't eat the pie because of all the hard pits.

Will You Trust Me?, p. 124
1. The Sacrament of Anointing of the Sick
2. Light
3. Jesus

Too Much of a Good Thing, p. 131
1. Seth ate too much pizza!
2. No.
3. Seth could have eaten a reasonable amount of pizza.
4. ...enjoy the good things that God has given us.

He Saw, and He Knows, p. 135
1. Becca cleaned the bathroom sinks.
2. Meg
3. Seth
4. Greg
5. Becca and Meg

Sharing 'Most Everything, p. 141
1. Becca didn't go to Mass because she had a cold.
2. ...of each other more than you think of yourselves.
3. One child cuts the treat in half, and the other child gets to pick which half.
To Think About: Becca caught Greg's cold.

Steps Leading Nowhere, p. 146
1. Dad drew guidelines to make it easier for Greg to build a treehouse.
2. ...expect that it will be all right in the end.

Big Rivers to Cross, p. 152
1. ...try.
2. Meg thought that she would drown.
3. Meg was not alone. Dad and Jesus were with her.
4. Meg remembered what Dad had read from The King of the Golden City, that Jesus would help her.
5. Jesus came to Meg in Holy Communion.

Because They Do, p. 158
1. Butchie hoped that he could get some pieces of barbecued meat.
2. Butchie scratched the screen door so someone would let him in the house.

Home, Sweet Home, p. 162
1. There were only four boys at Seth's camp-over because all the rest of his friends were busy with sports or other activities.

Looking Inside, p. 168
1. Greg shared his bubbles with Becca.
2. Greg tried to save Mother some time by cutting his own hair.

Joy to My Youth, p. 173
1. Nate had served eight times.
2. Nate served more than he was scheduled because the boys who were scheduled had not come.
3. a holy card of St. John Berchmans
4. ...no matter what.
5. changing hearts and saving souls.

A Gift that Won't Break, p. 179
1. look with his eyes, not his hands.
2. self-control
3. save souls

Squeaky Clean, p. 183
1. Greg got dirty climbing the pine tree.
2. Mother thought that Greg would like to wash his hair with the new banana-scented shampoo.
3. ...He sees and knows everything.

Hide and Seek, p. 188
Answers will vary.

Topical Index

activities, extracurricular: p. 162
Advent: p. 61, 74
altar boys: p. 173
anger: p. 11
appearances: p. 168
appetites, proper use of: p. 131
authority, in family: p. 46
children as blessings: p. 106
children, training: p. 158
chores: p. 95
Christmas: p. 74
Church teaching, following: p. 146
confession: p. 6, 67, 184
consequences: p. 67
contentment: p. 41
courage: p. 152
criticism: p. 118
discipline: p. 158
Epiphany: p. 74
Eucharist: p. 152
example, good: p. 56
Faith, living the: p. 106, 112
families, God's gift of: p. 29
family, priority of: p. 162
feelings vs. Truth: p. 20
forgiveness: p. 11
friends, choosing good: p. 20
friends, godly: p. 1
God, always with us: p. 25, 61
God, finding: p. 188
God, trust in: p. 124, 188
good, discerning: p. 20
grumbling: p. 95
heart, God sees inside: p. 168
honesty p. 36, 67, 99
imitating Jesus, saints: p. 56
Jesus, our strength: p. 152
judgment: p. 118
laziness: p. 99
Lent: p. 124, 135
lying: p. 99
Mass, Holy—attendance: p. 85
Mass, Holy Sacrifice of: p. 173
Mercy, Corporal Works of: p. 61
obedience: p. 36, 46
Obligation, Holy Days of: p. 85
offering up: p. 179
parents' instruction, following: p. 146
patience: p. 90
permission, asking: p. 99
perseverance: p. 152
pouting: p. 41
practice: p. 90
pro-life: p. 25
sacrifices: p. 135
Saints, Communion of: p. 124
self-control p. 16, 179
sharing: p. 141
sin, or accident:: p. 80
sin, consequences of: p. 67
speech, control of p. 16
speech, kindly: p. 141
sports: p. 162
stealing: p. 36
talents, using for God's glory: p. 51
talking back: p. 46
temptation: p. 36, 179
thankfulness: p. 41
whining: p. 41
work, independent: p. 95

Distributed by

Catholic Heritage Curricula

P.O. Box 125, Twain Harte, California 95383

To request a free catalog, call toll-free: 1-800-490-7713
Or visit online: www.chcweb.com

If your family enjoyed and benefited from these stories, perhaps you would also enjoy some of CHC's other homeschooling materials, whether for extra practice outside of school, homeschooling, or character development.

Other titles by Nancy Nicholson:
  Devotional Stories for Little Folks
  Little Folks' Letter Practice
  Little Folks' Number Practice
  Little Stories for Little Folks: Catholic Phonics Readers
  My Catholic Speller Series
  Langauge of God Series
  Easy As 1, 2, 3: A Catholic Overview of Science
  Catholic Stories from Science
  High School of Your Dreams

Other titles available from Catholic Heritage Curricula:
  The King of the Golden City by Mother Mary Loyola
  A Catholic How-To-Draw by Andrea Smith
  A Year with God: Celebrating the Liturgical Year
  Sewing with Saint Anne by Alice Cantrell
  Stories of the Saints: Volumes I-IV by Elaine Woodfield
  Behold and See: Beginning Science by Suchi Myjak
  And more